Isabel Somerset.

Engelberg, Switzerland

July, 1893.

Read on the Woman

Question p. 16 +

118 + 136

138 ~ 159 —

THE PROMOTION OF

GENERAL HAPPINESS

A UTILITARIAN ESSAY

BY

MICHAEL MACMILLAN, B.A., Oxon.

FELLOW OF THE BOMBAY UNIVERSITY, AND PROFESSOR OF LOGIC AND MORAL PHILOSOPHY
AT ELPHINSTONE COLLEGE, BOMBAY

We cannot expect to agree in our utilitarian estimates, at least without much debate. We must agree to differ, and though we are bound to argue fearlessly, it should be with the consciousness that there is room for wide and *bonâ fide* difference of opinion. We must consent to advance cautiously, step by step, feeling our way, adopting no foregone conclusions, trusting no single science, expecting no infallible guide.— JEVONS : *The State in Relation to Labour.*

LONDON
SWAN SONNENSCHEIN & CO.
PATERNOSTER SQUARE
1890

PREFACE.

In the following pages I have borrowed from Professor Henry Sidgwick the useful word "felicific," and doubtless I have in many passages been consciously or unconsciously influenced by the same writer. It would indeed have been impossible for me to read his *Methods of Ethics* for ten successive years in the ordinary routine of my Indian work, each year with increased admiration for the Aristotelian thoroughness of the discussions it contains, without having my opinions on many subjects, and my way of looking at all questions, considerably affected thereby.

SUMMARY OF CONCLUSIONS.

CHAPTER I.

PAGE

GENERAL REMARKS.—Even if happiness entirely depended on comparison of our own possessions with those of others, happiness might be increased (1) by discovery of a more miserable race of beings, (2) by spread of pessimistic ideas. So far as it depends on comparison with previous generations, it can be increased by the discovery of new sources of pleasure. So far as it depends on comparison with our own past state, it may be increased by sudden increase of production or discovery of new sources of pleasure. But happiness is not always due to comparison, and therefore other sources of happiness must be considered. Custom blunts our sensibility to pleasure and pain, but does not make it impossible to increase or decrease general happiness. We must assume, unless there is reason to the contrary, that the increase of any individual's happiness increases general happiness 1

CHAPTER II.

KNOWLEDGE AND EDUCATION.—Knowledge being imperfect cannot give mental satisfaction, nor can mankind by increase of knowledge gain happiness through a feeling of superiority, nor can greater knowledge of the world's condition be assumed to be productive of happiness unless we accept optimism. Increase of knowledge will direct aright utilitarian action, and will be expected by the utilitarian to lead to the more general adoption of utilitarianism. It will also prevent useless riots and rebellions. The spread of female education should be especially encouraged by the utilitarian as the best remedy for the infelicific inequality between the sexes 12

CHAPTER III.

INVENTIVE KNOWLEDGE.—The power over nature given by knowledge being still imperfect gives no more mental satisfaction

JUL 20 1961

CHAPTER VII.

CHAPTER VIII.

CHAPTER IX.

CHAPTER X.

THE

PROMOTION OF GENERAL HAPPINESS

~·<♡º©·~·

CHAPTER I.

UTILITARIANS regard the increase of the happiness of the
world as the only reasonable end of conduct, as the only
object desirable in itself. According to them even virtue
itself would not be desirable unless it promoted the
happiness of the world, and, if it had the contrary effect,
would be the reverse of desirable. This extreme opinion
is only held by a fraction of civilised men, a large
number of whom consider that not only virtue but also
knowledge and art are desirable for their own sake. But
even those who regard virtue, knowledge, art and other
objects as desirable for their own sakes regard general
happiness as also desirable for its own sake. Some might
possibly prefer or think they prefer in certain cases increase of virtue, knowledge, and art to increase of happiness, but, if they saw that a certain action would increase
happiness and would have no prejudicial results in any
other directions, they would think such an action ought
to be done. Even the sternest moralists and religious
teachers, who show us the admirable discipline afforded
by pain, do not appear to be exceptions. For, though
they think pain sometimes desirable in the interests of
virtue and religion, they would prefer happiness if it

A

were equally conducive to the same end. If beautiful
music promoted virtue as much as a trying bodily disease, who would not prefer the former to the latter?
Thus it appears that everyone, or at any rate everyone
whose opinion is worth taking into consideration, prefers
general happiness to general misery either absolutely or
cæteris paribus. Therefore we may well consider it a
question of universal interest whether the general happiness can be promoted by any means, and if so, by what
means.

There is one general argument against the possibility
of promoting happiness, which, if accepted, will finally
close the question we are considering. It may be argued
that all happiness depends upon comparison of one's own
possessions with another's, that, if a man is happy, it
must be because he possesses or thinks he possesses a
larger supply of health, wealth and other generally desired objects than other men have. If this is the whole
truth of the matter, it might be argued that no human
effort can increase the happiness of the world. Certainly
in that case it would be useless to try to increase the
world's happiness by making the human race wealthier,
healthier, or longer lived. Under the supposition the
human race would be thereby no more benefited than the
candidates in a competitive examination would be by having all their marks doubled. Nevertheless, there would
still be other conceivable means by which happiness might
be increased. Supposing the human race could become
firmly convinced of the existence of some other previously
unknown class of beings, say, the inhabitants of another
planet less provided with the usual objects of desire than
themselves, then the happiness of the human race would
be increased, as the happiness of the saints is supposed
by some of the ancient fathers to be enhanced by contemplation of the punishment of the damned. But this
discovery must not be mutual or else happiness would
still remain unaffected. For the happiness of the in-

habitants of the other planet would be decreased by the discovery as much as the happiness of the human race would be increased, and the positive and negative quantities would cancel each other. Therefore the utilitarian would have to do his best to defend the inhabitants of the less fortunate planet against the infelicific consequences which would result to them from the knowledge of our better fortunes. But owing to the little probability of being able to discover a new unknown race of beings, and the equal probability of such a race if discovered being more and not less fortunately circumstanced than the human race, the utilitarian, convinced of the comparative nature of happiness, would try to find other means to increase it. He would perhaps try to affect not the facts contemplated but the contemplating mind, and would strive to divert his fellow men from the contemplation of those superior to themselves in the possession of objects of desire, to the contemplation of the many who suffer most from poverty, disease and other evils. Much might be done by disseminating among the multitude at cheap prices the works of Voltaire, Leopardi, Schopenhauer and other pessimists, in order that by reading their descriptions of the misery of the human race, and recognising themselves to be less miserable than the average human being is supposed to be by philosophic observers who have carefully studied the matter, they might feel their superiority over the average man and thereby become happier.

So far we have been considering the consequences that would follow if happiness depended entirely on comparison of one's own condition with that of contemporary men. We also sometimes compare our condition with that of previous generations, and this comparison affects happiness to a certain limited extent. So far as this is the case, it is possible for ordinary human effort to increase happiness by, for instance, endowing each successive generation with sources of pleasure unknown before or with an additional supply of the old sources. For thus men would see that they have sources of pleasure unknown to their ancestors, and would derive pleasure from the fact. This consideration is however, though worth noticing, not important, as men are much more apt to compare themselves with their contemporaries whom they see around them every day, than with their forbears whose lives they dimly realise through the medium of books and traditions.

But there is a different kind of comparison on which happiness depends. Men may be happy not merely because they compare themselves with other men and think themselves happier, but also because they compare their present state with a previous state in which they were less happy. The human race has often anticipated and repeated Dante's judgment that the greatest grief is to remember in misery past happiness. It is equally true that happiness is intensified by comparison with one's own past misery. Virgil makes storm-tost Æneas look forward to a time when the agonies endured in a tempestuous sea will be a subject for pleasant reflection, and the number of times that the words,

Forsitan haec olim meminisse juvabit,

have been since quoted shows that the truth of the idea has been generally recognised. This same close connection between pleasure and pain had been recognised long before by Plato. Socrates, in the *Phædo*, being released from his chain as a preliminary to his execution, remarks : " How singular is the thing called pleasure, and how curiously related to pain, which might be thought to be the opposite of it ; for they never will come to a man together, and yet he who pursues either of them is generally compelled to take the other. Their bodies are two, and yet they are joined to a single head ; and I cannot help thinking that if Æsop had noticed them, he would have made a fable about God trying to reconcile their strife, and how, when he could not, he fastened their heads together ; and this is the reason why when one comes the other follows, as I find in my own case pleasure comes following after the pain in my leg which was caused by the chain." [1] The fact of the origination of happiness from such comparison of one's own past pain with present pleasure, like the comparison of the misery of past ages with present pleasure, is compatible with the increase of general happiness by human effort. But it affords the means of increasing general happiness to a much greater extent. For men much more often and more vividly compare their present state with their own past state than their state with the state of previous generations of mankind. If the whole human race or any portion of it, owing to the discovery of some new agricultural or other productive machine, increase the production of the earth, and consequently are much less pressed for want of food than they were a few years before, the consequent comparison of present plenty with past want decidedly increases happiness for the time, that is until increase of population restores the normal state of want. The discovery of new sources of pleasure will have the same effect. Thus, so far as human happiness depends upon this kind of comparison, ordinary human effort in the invention of new pleasures and in the increase of man's power over nature increases happiness.

We have now seen that of the three ways in which comparison effects happiness only the first reveals a source of happiness which almost entirely mocks utilitarian effort. It will be shown further on in detail how the consideration of the very large extent to which happiness depends on this first kind of comparison interferes with the happiness which would otherwise be secured by the progress of mechanical science. But we have also seen that the effects of the other two kinds of com-

[1] Jowett's Plato.

parison are not so disheartening to the utilitarian. And after all there are many other sources of happiness besides these three kinds of comparison. In fact if we consider the matter carefully we shall find that comparison rather intensifies than originates pleasure and pain. Comparison is strongest and most frequent when we rise to the full grown civilised man, the highest point in the evolutional scale. In his case, no doubt, each pleasure is often intensified by comparison with past pain or with the pain suffered by other men. But it is merely a case of intensification, not of origination. If comparison were the only source of pleasure, the reflective man would enjoy far more and far keener happiness than the animal world. But this does not seem to be the case, but rather the contrary. The happiness enjoyed by the lowest classes of living beings it is hard or impossible to estimate. Ants, and bees, and flies, and worms, still more such minute organisms as bacteria, are so unlike us that we cannot interpret their signs of emotion. But when we come to the consideration of the animals whose feelings we can more easily conjecture, they seem to enjoy keener or at least as keen pleasure as human beings. The pig at his trough, the dog leaping wildly in anticipation of a walk with his master, the horse galloping over green turf all seem to show manifestations of greater joy than that of which their lords are capable. So does the unreflective child, although he, like the pig, the dog, and the horse, is for the most part absorbed in the present moment and is not readily inclined to think of the happiness of other children. But if the premisses of this argument are not convincing, if it is thought that, after all, the undemonstrative civilised man enjoys greater pleasure than the child with joy beaming in its face or than the dog expressing its exuberant delight by bounding and barking, we must appeal to our own consciousness to settle the question. Do we always, whenever we feel happy, contrast our present state with our own different state in the past or

with that of other people ? Surely we must answer this
question in the negative. The man with a good appetite
enjoying a good dinner does not necessarily at the moment
of enjoyment think of hungry men or of his own previous
hungry state. The virtuous man can feel the glow of
self-approbation consequent on a good act without making a comparison in his own favour of himself with other
less virtuous men, nor does he think of other moments
of his life when he was not engaged in virtuous action.
Indeed, if he did make such comparisons, they would
cause him pain rather than pleasure. Nor does the
astronomer, into whose ken some new planet swims,
make any such comparison when he is full of the joy of
his great discovery. If he does, it is rather an after-
thought, a possible concomitant of his elevated pleasure,
than the cause of that pleasure. Thus we may easily
convince ourselves that happiness is not altogether the
result of comparison. And even if it were, it is clear
from the consideration of the three kinds of comparison
affecting happiness that the general happiness would not
be as impracticable an object of endeavour as perpetual
motion or the construction of a triangle with its three
angles less than two right angles. Nevertheless, as we
consider the various sources of happiness we shall find
that again and again the promotion of the general happiness is retarded and rendered impossible by the strong
inclination that men have to continually compare their
own position with that of their fellowmen and by the all
powerful effect on happiness which necessarily follows
from this comparison.

Another objection to the possibility of affecting happiness, rests on the effects of custom. There is a vulgar
saying, that we can get used to anything as eels get
used to being skinned. Mammon in the great debate
held at Pandemonium, discussing the practicability of
obtaining happiness among the fires of hell, plausibly
remarks :

> "Our torments also may, in length of time,
> Become our elements, these piercing fires
> As soft as now severe, our temper changed
> Into their temper ; which must needs remove
> The sensible of pain."

Experience gives support to these views. H. Drummond, speaking of the *Ilala* steamer which plies on the shores of the African Lake of Nyassa, ten degrees south of the equator, remarks : " Singularly enough, while deck hands are often enlisted after some persuasion, the competition for the office of fireman—a disagreeable post at any time, but in the tropical heat the last to be coveted —is so keen that any number of natives are at all times ready to be frizzled in the stoke hole. Instead of avoiding heat, the African native everywhere courts it. His nature expands and revels in it; while a breath of cold on a mountain slope, or a sudden shower of rain, transforms him instantly into a most woebegone object." On the other hand, we find many strong Northerners like Kingsley who revel in the cold blasts of a British north easter. In war, soldiers become accustomed to continual danger and the frequent deaths of their comrades. In bombarded towns, civilians and women come to look with indifference upon bursting shells. Many instances might be quoted of persons who, though their life was one long disease, yet reconciled themselves to their situation and seemed to enjoy as much happiness as their neighbours. Even leprosy can lose its horrors from familiarity. Travellers who have visited the leper settlement at Molakai in the Pacific, describe the inhabitants as not utterly miserable, although they are all doomed to die of their loathsome disease sooner or later. On the other hand, familiarity also breeds contempt for sources of pleasure. Most boys thoroughly enjoy eating jam tarts. But allow a boy to eat jam tarts at every meal in the day, and he will soon cease to regard them as very delightful.

There is, then, no doubt that familiarity does in a wonderful way blunt our sensibility to sources of pleasure and sources of pain, and this fact tends to make the balance of happiness throughout the world far more equal than it would otherwise be. But it by no means produces perfect equality of happiness. It may, indeed, in some cases, produce inequality. By the operation of this law, the unfortunate man who always suffers from the same pain, is less unhappy than the unfortunate man who is always plunging out of the frying pan into the fire, and so varying his sources of pain. On the other hand, the fortunate man may increase his happiness through knowledge of this law by continually varying his pleasures. On this account Mill recommends variation between the pleasures of repose and the pleasures of activity, as the best means of securing happiness. Also there are, no doubt, many sources of pleasure that are always pleasant. A healthy man may all through his life at every meal derive real enjoyment from his food, even though each meal may not give him quite as much pleasure as it would give a man who has never sat down to a good meal. And it is the same with many sources of pain. It is quite possible for a deaf man to go on being irritated every day in his life by his failure to hear properly what is being said in his presence. Custom does much to alleviate the pain of the unfortunate, and to lessen the pleasure of the fortunate, but it is far from producing a dead level of happiness among all the members of the human race and of the brute creation. In spite of the effect of custom, it is quite possible for one man to be happier than another, and for the average happiness at one time to be greater than at another time.

After this preliminary discussion we may proceed to discuss the various means by which men confidently hope that the general happiness may be promoted.

Before going farther it is, however, necessary if possible to remove ambiguity in the terms of the discussion, such as is so frequently due to the confusion of individual and general happiness, against which we are warned by Mr. Henry Sidgwick in his *Methods of Ethics.* In the following pages, happiness, when used without quali-fication, will mean the general happiness of all sentient beings, which may, of course, be promoted by increase of the happiness of one individual, if such increase is not secured at the expense of the happiness of others. Thus, if I make myself or any other individual happier, and see no reason to believe that my or his gain is some other man's loss, I naturally assume that not only one individual's happiness, but also happiness without qualifi-cation is promoted. The same assumption must be made with regard to the happiness of unknown creatures of other worlds, if such there be. By promoting happiness in this world we either do not affect at all the happiness of other worlds, or, if we do, we are so entirely unable to calculate whether our actions will affect the happiness of those other worlds favourably or unfavourably, that, as reasonable beings, we leave such possible effects out of consideration, just as we very often leave out of consider-ation, owing to similar ignorance, the effect of our actions on beings of this world. For instance, a utilitarian in choosing his residence knows that his choice will affect the happiness of the various tradesmen living round the two houses one of which he intends to select. If he settles at A, he will by his custom affect the happiness of the tradesmen of A ; and if he settles at B, he will affect the happiness of the tradesmen of that town. But as he pro-bably has no possible data to determine whether the tradesmen of A or of B would derive more happiness from his settling in their midst, he will leave all this out of consideration, and confine his calculations to the effect likely to be produced on the happiness of himself, his relations and friends. When effects are so unknown as to be beyond the power of our intelligence to calculate, and others are well enough known to be estimable by experience, we disregard the former and determine our conduct entirely by the latter. If, following this method of exclusion, we fall into results that we did not desire, we do not incur the charge of folly. Suppose that, of two men equally desirous to reach the same destination, one chooses the road that he knows to be hillier and longer, while the other chooses the shorter and more level road, the latter shows himself by his choice to be the wiser of the two, even though, owing to circumstances which neither of them had any possible means of calculating beforehand, he is gored to death on his way by a mad bull, and never reaches his destination.

CHAPTER II.

LET us begin by trying to estimate how far happiness can be increased by increasing knowledge. This enquiry naturally divides itself into two parts. We must first consider whether the mere possession of knowledge makes each individual happier, and then whether the results of knowledge increase the happiness of the multitude of ignorant and learned who make use of these results.

In considering the former part of the question we are immediately met by the difficulty arising from the imperfection of knowledge. Various degrees of knowledge are after all only more or less near approximations to ignorance. The most learned man more clearly recognises his real ignorance than the untaught clown. Newton describes himself as like a child picking up a few shells by the seashore of knowledge. Not only experience but all knowledge is " an arch wherethrough gleams that untravelled world whose margin fades for ever and for ever as we move." Therefore, as far as the consciousness of having everything explained to one's satisfaction is concerned, the self-confident village ignoramus is often better off than the profoundest philosopher who ever tried and tried in vain to solve the riddle of the universe.

Perhaps the happiest of all then are those who have never desired any more knowledge than that which enables them to live. Men in such a condition are entirely free from the feelings of dissatisfaction felt by those who would like to know everything and are dis-

appointed of their ardent desire for perfect knowledge.
Intelligent observers have imagined that they found the
greatest happiness among the South Sea Islanders and
other ignorant men, if only they live in a fertile country
under sunny skies. The negroes of the West Indian
islands are very destitute of anything that we should
call knowledge, yet Mr. Froude gives a most glowing
account of their happiness. "They are," he writes,
"perfectly happy. In no part of the globe is there any
peasantry whose every want is so completely satisfied as
Her Majesty's black subjects in these West Indian
Islands. They have no aspirations to make them restless. They have no guilt upon their consciences. They
have food for the picking up. Clothes they need not,
and lodging in such a climate need not be elaborate.
They have perfect liberty and are safe from dangers, to
which if left to themselves they would be exposed, for
the English rule prevents the strong from oppressing the
weak. In their own country they would have remained
slaves to the more warlike races. In the West Indies
their fathers underwent a bondage of a century or two,
lighter at its worst than the earliest form of it in Africa;
their descendants in return have nothing now to do save
to laugh and sing and enjoy existence. Their quarrels,
if they have any, begin and end in words. If happiness
is the be all and end all of life, and those who have most
of it have most completely attained the object of their
being, the 'nigger' who now basks among the ruins of
the West Indian plantations is the supremest specimen
of present humanity." Or hear the description of this
same race of men in a still more ignorant state before
they have been torn away from their native soil. "Here
in his virgin simplicity," says H. Drummond, describing
his central African experiences, " dwells primeval man,
without clothes, without civilisation, without learning,
without religion—the genuine child of nature, thought-
less, careless and contented. This man is apparently

quite happy; he has practically no wants." Such men have never been much troubled by unsatisfied yearnings for knowledge. Confining our attention to those who have had such yearnings, we have no reason to believe that the world in the nineteenth century enjoys more mental satisfaction from its greater but imperfect knowledge than any previous century derived from its lesser knowledge. Therefore, it seems plain that the increase of knowledge does simply nothing to remove the unhappiness of mental unrest, and will do nothing unless it becomes absolutely perfect. But, as far as we can see, absolutely perfect knowledge is beyond the reach of human endeavour.

It may, however, be urged that, though the learned man is equally dissatisfied or more dissatisfied with his ignorance than the unlearned, he will be rendered happier by the consciousness of superiority. This is true with limitations. The unlearned man often thinks he knows more than the learned, and the learned man is often so modest that he is not conscious of his own superiority. But, nevertheless, as a rule not without exceptions it may be allowed that the unlearned man recognizes the superior knowledge of the learned man, and that the learned man recognizes his own superiority. Therefore, as the feeling of superiority gives happiness, this fact tends to make the learned man happier than the unlearned. Here, however, we have individual happiness due to comparison of a man with his fellowmen, which scarcely ever, as we have seen, affords a fulcrum for raising the general happiness to a greater height. However much we increase the knowledge of the world, there will always be, as far as we can see, a certain fraction of mankind superior to the average in knowledge, and another probably equal fraction inferior to the average. The happiness of superiority in knowledge can scarcely be enjoyed by more than half of the human race, and the most successful effort to increase knowledge only raises the standard of average knowledge, and so makes more knowledge to be required to gain that superiority of knowledge which constitutes happiness.

It may, however, be supposed that knowledge in another way promotes happiness, that a wide intelligent survey of the universe shows a great predominance of happiness over misery, and that he who can make such a survey will enjoy happiness through sympathy with his happy fellow men and fellow creatures. This however can only be an *argumentum ad hominem.* It will be convincing to the optimist, but excite the scorn of the pessimist. There are probably as many pessimists as optimists in the world, and most men steer a middle course between these two doctrines, being optimists in good health, and pessimists when they suffer from derangement of the liver or toothache. The majority of mankind will have to be convinced of the truth of optimism before they can be expected to allow that extended knowledge gives clearer recognition of the happiness of the world.

Thus it appears plain that the mere possession of knowledge cannot be clearly seen by any one but a confirmed optimist to promote happiness. We must therefore now consider whether the results of knowledge are such as to promote happiness.

In the first place it is clear that, if it is possible to promote happiness by human action, the increase of knowledge on the part of utilitarians will enable them to carry out this desirable object more successfully. For by increase of knowledge they will see more clearly by what means the great end at which they aim may be best attained. Also the utilitarian will expect that increase of knowledge will lead to the more universal adoption of utilitarian morality. So that for those two reasons, he will be inclined to support the cause of education and spread knowledge over the world with all his power.

There is also a strong political argument in favour of education. It is popularly supposed that education increases the tendency to riots, rebellion and sedition. This popular fallacy may best be answered in the words of Bacon, who remarks that " to say that a blind custom of obedience should be a surer obligation than duty taught and understood, is to affirm that a blind man may tread surer by a guide than a seeing man can by a light. And it is without all controversy that learning doth make the minds of men gentle, generous, maniable, and pliant to government; whereas ignorance makes them churlish, thwart and mutinous; and the evidence of time doth clear this assertion, considering that the most barbarous, rude, and unlearned times have been most subject to tumults, seditions, and changes." The frequency of the delusion combated by Bacon is due to the fact that education affords the means by which discontent is clearly expressed in words, and conveys the knowledge of every riot and insurrection rapidly all over the globe. Owing to the energy of the newspaper press and the large number of those who can now read newspapers, persons not endowed with reflection think that there are far more riots and rebellions than there used to be. But a short comparison of the destruction of life and property in late riots and rebellions and in those of an earlier uneducated age would soon dissipate that idea, and would also make clear that destructive riots and foolish rebellions have been chiefly made by the uneducated masses. Ignorance has led to many hopeless uprisings prompted often not by wrong but by ignorant fanaticism. In English history the Gordon riots and the Rebecca riots are good illustrations of this. India has lately given a conspicuous instance on a small scale of the same fact in the rebellion of a few hundred fanatics at Broach, who thought that they could overthrow the British Government, and believed their leader's promise, that his prayer would render the bullets of the sepoys as harmless as peas. Such uprisings prompted by ignorance lead to much misery by destruction of life and property, and usually do nothing to help the great struggle against unjust oppression. The utilitarian will also with especial zeal support the cause of female education. For now, as in the past, deficiency of education is one of the chief means by which woman is kept in a more or less subservient position throughout the world. Everything that tends to inequality is prejudicial to happiness, because the inferior feels more pain at his inferiority than the pleasure afforded to the superior by his sense of superiority. Also power over inferiors is bad for the moral condition, and therefore, as we shall see later, for the happiness of both inferiors and superiors. This is peculiarly manifest in the effect that is produced on women and men by the inequality of law and custom in the various countries of the world and especially in the East. The greater this inequality is, the more tyrannical man becomes, and the more servile or cunning woman becomes. The history of civilisation has on the whole displayed a tendency towards improvement in the condition of woman. But this tendency to progress has not been without exception. Women were more free and more nearly in a position of equality to men in pre-historic Greece than in the more civilised times of Pericles and Demosthenes, and are less free in Modern India than in the state of society depicted in the old Indian Epics Mahometanism, even when in other respects it has been a civilising influence, has always lowered the status of women by polygamy and seclusion. But generally speaking, the position of women has advanced with the progress of centuries. In the United States, the most modern of the powers of the world, woman has most nearly secured her complete emancipation, and for striking instances of her subjection we must look for the most part to ancient times, and barbarous or half-civilised communities.

B

We read in the pages of Abbé Raynal that savage mothers on the banks of the Orinoco justified female infanticide on the ground of the overwhelming wretchedness of female life. One of them reproached with this crime by a Jesuit father replied, "Represent to thyself, O Father, the troubles that are reserved for an Indian woman among these Indians. They accompany us into the fields with their bow and arrows ; while we go there laden with an infant whom we carry in a basket, and another who hangs at our breast. They go to kill birds or to catch fish, while we are employed in digging the ground, and, after having gone through all the labours of the culture, are obliged also to bear those of the harvest. They return in the evening without any burthen, and we bring them roots for their food, and maize for their drink. As soon as they come home, they go and amuse themselves with their friends ; while we are fetching wood and water to prepare for their supper. When they have eaten, they fall asleep ; and we pass almost the whole night in grinding the maize and in preparing the chica for them. And what reward have we for these labours ? They drink : and when they are intoxicated, they drag us by the hair, and trample us under foot. . . . . . It is a melancholy circumstance for a poor Indian woman to serve her husband as a slave in the fields, oppressed with fatigue and at home deprived of tranquillity, but it is a dreadful thing when twenty years are elapsed, to see him take another woman, whose judgment is not formed. He attaches himself to her. She beats our children ; she commands us, and treats us as her servants ; and, if the least murmur escape us, a stick raised. . . . . Oh ! Father, how is it possible that we should bear this condition ?   What can an Indian woman do better than to prevent her child from living in a state of slavery worse than death ? " This gives a sad but true picture of the way in which women are usually treated in the lowest stage of civilisation, when the rights of the sexes are settled entirely by brute force. Not much better seems to have been the position of women in ancient Greece and in modern and ancient oriental states; for freedom from hard work in the fields is dearly purchased by richer women in the East at the expense of the loss of their freedom of motion in the open air. In many other respects in the East, law and custom make unjust distinctions between men and women. In India a man may take a second wife if his first wife dies or even if she is childless. But as a rule a woman is never allowed to take a second husband, even if her first died when she was a mere child. On the contrary, it was considered proper for a virtuous widow to burn herself with her husband's corpse, and if she failed to do so became degraded for life. Since suttee has been declared illegal by the British Government, it is now rarely practised, but the indignities to which widows are subjected by custom still remain and make many women regret that the law compels them to survive their husbands.

Among some of the tribes that inhabit Madagascar, women are treated with the same kind of injustice that they too often suffer in India. The Mahafali, we read, consider the woman as an inferior being, bound to perform all her duties towards man, but enjoying no rights. The wife is not allowed to eat with her husband, and, when she dies, her corpse is not carried to the sacred ground reserved for him. Among the Sihanaka, widows are treated with savage brutality. "Upon the death of any man of position or wealth," we read in Sibree's Madagascar, "on the day of the funeral the wife is placed in the house, dressed in all her best clothes, and covered with her silver ornaments, of which the Sihanaka wear a considerable quantity. There she remains until the rest of the family return home from the tomb. But as soon as they enter the house, they begin to revile her with most abusive language, telling her that it is her fault that her vintana or fate has been stronger than that of her husband. They then strip her of her clothes, tearing off with violence the ornaments from her ears and neck, and arms; they give her a coarse cloth, a spoon with a broken handle, and a dish with the foot broken off with which to eat; her hair is dishevelled, and she is covered up with a coarse mat, and under that she remains all day long, and can only leave it at night; and she may not speak to any one who goes into the house. She is not allowed to wash her face or hands, but only the tips of her fingers. She endures all this sometimes for a year, or, at least, for eight months." For all the oppression and degradation of women in the East, and the inequality of their privileges as compared with men in the West, the remedy is to be found in the improvement of the quantity and quality of female education, which will not only emancipate them from their position of inferiority, but also fit them for the higher and more independent position they may expect to have in the more perfect civilisation of the future.

The same good result is promoted, though in a less degree, by general progress in education. The more educated a nation becomes, the less men are inclined to tyrannise over women by means of their superiority in physical strength, and the greater is the tendency to distribute honour and privileges according to mental excellence. In general ability woman is inferior to man, as was admitted by the staunchest upholder of women's rights in ancient times. "Can you mention," asks Socrates in the fifth book of the Republic, "any pursuit of man, in which the male sex has not all these qualities (natural gifts) in a far higher degree than the female? Need I waste time in speaking of the art of weaving and the management of pancakes and preserves, in which womankind does really appear to be great, and in which for her to be beaten is the most absurd of all things?" To which Glaucon replies: "You are quite right in maintaining the general inferiority of the female sex; at the same time many women are in many things superior to many men, though, speaking generally, what you say is true." The cleverest woman is inferior to the cleverest man, and the average woman is inferior to the average man. But this inferiority has been as a rule grossly exaggerated, and, being ~~partially~~ due to neglect or misdirection of female education in the past, will be much diminished when women are as well taught as men. At any rate it is plain that woman is less inferior to man in mental than in bodily power, and, as the general progress of education causes increased importance and honour to be attached to mental excellence, it is sure to do much to improve the position of women, and so, by removing or diminishing inequality, will promote general happiness. ✗

✗ Men first debase women for illimitable centuries & then quietly pronounce them 'inferior'. This process of thought does little credit to their (men's) powers of just reasoning from Socrates down. Selah.

CHAPTER III.

WE must now turn to the consideration of the more material effects of knowledge. It has been said with truth, that knowledge is power, and the power that knowledge has put into the hands of man has altered the face of the earth, and in a wonderful way changed the conditions of existence for the human race. That this mighty change has been immensely productive of happiness seems to be very generally accepted. The opinions of those who believe this are eloquently and confidently expressed by Macaulay in his eulogium of the Baconian philosophy.

The follower of Bacon being asked what his philosophy has effected for mankind is made to say, "It has lengthened life; it has mitigated pain; it has extinguished diseases; it has increased the fertility of the soil; it has given new securities to the mariner; it has furnished new arms to the warrior; it has spanned great rivers and estuaries with bridges of form unknown to our fathers; it has guided the thunderbolt innocuously from heaven to earth; it has lighted up the night with the splendour of the day; it has extended the range of the human vision; it has multiplied the power of the human muscles; it has accelerated motion; it has annihilated distance; it has facilitated intercourse, correspondence, all friendly offices, all despatch of business; it has enabled man to descend to the depths of the sea, to soar into the air, to penetrate securely into the noxious recesses of the earth, to traverse the land in cars which whirl along without horses, and the ocean in ships which run ten knots an hour against the wind. These are but a part of its fruits and of its first fruits."

This is all very true. The philosophy of invention has produced wonderful results. But what is the good of it all, if it does not add to the sum of human happiness? If it is said that it brings man nearer to perfection thus to conquer nature, we are inclined to reply that Zoroaster upon Ushidarema or Buddha pondering under the sacred fig tree over the mystery of life, was perhaps a grander being than the most skilful engine-driver who ever controlled the speed of the Flying Scotchman. But here we have been tempted for a moment to diverge from the line of our enquiry. What we have proposed to ourselves is a consideration of the possibility of increasing, not excellence, but happiness. Only if excellence or approach to perfection makes the possessor or other men happier, does it come within the scope of our enquiry? Now it seems that excellence can only promote the happiness of the excellent or perfect person by satisfying pride or by removing the restless craving for greater excellence. The satisfaction of pride based on greater power over nature than is enjoyed by one's fellowmen, may perhaps increase the happiness of individuals, but we have seen that it can scarcely increase the happiness of the race, as this feeling of superiority was enjoyed by as large a fraction of mankind when the greatest products of inventive skill were wooden ploughs, flint heads, and bows and arrows, as in the present century of Eiffel Towers, Suez Canals, Cunard steamers, and phonographs. Nor can the age or the individuals who produce such works of power as we now see around us enjoy in any peculiar degree the satisfaction of victory over nature. The feeling of conquest was no doubt enjoyed with the same zest by the first constructor of a roofed hut, as by M. Eiffel when his iron tower reached its destined height. For the joy lies in the progress achieved. The first hut was surely as great an advance on the primeval cave, as the Eiffel Tower is an improvement on the towers of Notre Dame. Looked upon in comparison with the powers of nature, all human mechanical effort is alike insignificant and imperfect. We can divert them a little, and so make the outer skin of an atom in the universe a little different from what it would otherwise have been. But even in this limited sphere the power of man, even in the nineteenth century, is extremely limited, as is shown whenever earthquakes or inundations of tempests exert their destructive powers. And it is painfully evident that if some erratic heavenly body should come into collision with us and drive us into the sun, our poor little earth, bedizened with all the architectural, mechanical, and sartorial glories of the nineteenth century, would be reduced in a moment to a mass of hot matter indistinguishable from what the same world would have become, had it met with the same catastrophe before primeval man had emerged from his cave dwellings and clothed himself in the skins of slain animals.

But it will be answered that, though man is still infinitely removed from complete conquest of nature, all partial advances in this direction give him more satisfaction to his desires, more comfort, and therefore more happiness. This is in the main how Macaulay thought that the Baconian philosophy increased the happiness of the world. He and all who think with him, that is, he and the majority of practical men, suppose that mechanical inventions have done much in the past to increase happiness, and that the best way to get the same result in the future is to go on making such inventions. In Bacon's time the three inventions that most impressed his imagination and that of his contemporaries were gunpowder, printing, and the mariner's compass. These three inventions have probably had a greater effect in modifying the conditions of human existence than the steam engine or the electric telegraph or any subsequent invention. Let us then follow Bacon in taking them as typical examples of great inventions and considering how far they promote happiness.

Although something might be said for the felicific effects of gunpowder, and although Macaulay seems to count the new arms furnished to the warrior among the excellent gifts with which the Baconian philosophy has endowed mankind, it is hardly necessary seriously to discuss the claims of this invention to honour, from a hedonistic point of view. Gunpowder is used most extensively on the battle-field, and does not appear on the whole to have mitigated the horrors of war. If those horrors have been mitigated, the change has been due rather to moral improvement than to change in the weapons of destruction. A gunshot wound may possibly be less painful to the sense and less horrible to the imagination than a sword cut, spear thrust, or an arrow fixed in the flesh, but surely the sight of fellow soldiers mangled out of all resemblance to humanity by artillery and the fear of suffering the same in one's own body is worse than the ordinary incidents of ancient smokeless battlefields. So far as gunpowder is used for peaceful purposes in blasting, it can be considered together with the many other devices for increasing the productive power of human labour, of which devices the most indisputable effect is, as will presently be seen, increase in the population of the world. This increase of population is also one of the principal effects of the discovery of previously unknown parts of the world due to the invention of the mariner's compass. The other principal effect of ocean travelling is increase in knowledge, which, as we have seen, does not clearly promote happiness. Therefore in considering the mariner's compass we have chiefly to estimate the effect of increase of population on the world's happiness. There is no doubt that the mariner's compass has done much to increase the number of human beings. Had the

compass not been invented, America would never have
been discovered and peopled by civilised European immigrants, or would have been discovered later.   The
continent of America before its discovery can scarcely
have contained twenty millions of inhabitants.   As a
consequence of its discovery, it has now a population of
90,000,000, which may be expected in the course of time
to expand to 500,000,000.

This is truly a wonderful effect to have been produced by the discovery of the magnetic needle.   But
does such an increase of population add to the sum of
human happiness ?   In this case we have no reason to
believe that the increase of population has diminished
the happiness of the average man.   The European
settlers in America are, for anything one can see to the
contrary, as happy or not more miserable than the
aboriginal inhabitants whom they have displaced or reduced in numbers, until they have become a small minority
in the population of the continent of which they were
formerly the undisputed possessors.   Now, if the average
man before the increase of population due to the discovery of America, enjoyed 10 degrees of happiness, and
the world then contained 800,000,000 inhabitants, the
aggregate happiness enjoyed was 8,000,000,000 degrees.
If the discovery of America adds 500,000,000 to the
population of the human race without altering the
average happiness, it then adds 5,000,000,000 degrees of
happiness to the aggregate happiness of the human race.
But how, if the average happiness of man be more properly represented by a negative quantity ?   The philosophical world is pretty equally divided between optimists
and pessimists.   Those who hold the latter view should,
if consistent utilitarians, offer determined opposition to
any discovery tending to add to the number of miserable
beings in the world.   As for practical persons not addicted to deliberate reflection on the evils and joys of
life, they generally waver in the balance between

optimism and pessimism. Yet every utilitarian, nay, every one who thinks that happiness is among things desirable for their own sake, ought to make up his mind on this question, as its decision gives a most important motive for the determination of conduct. If the unknown inventor of the mariner's compass was a pessimistic utilitarian, and foresaw that his invention would add millions to the population of the world, he was bound as a rational being to keep his discovery to himself.

The same remarks apply to the invention of all other instruments which increase the world's population either by making the soil more productive, or by improving the means of communication between different parts of the world, so that each country produces what it can produce most easily, and gives its surplus to foreign nations in exchange for what they can produce most easily. For this increase of population is, after all, the principal result of steam-ploughs, steam-ships, steam-locomotives, and all the vaunted triumphs of steam. The population of England at the beginning of this century, was in round numbers 8,500,000, and in the fifty years between 1800 and 1850, rose to 16,000,000. This wonderful increase may almost entirely be attributed to the immense increase in productive power given to human labour by the use of steam-power; for a large number of modern inventions having the same effect were prompted by desire to utilise to the full the power of steam, and, therefore, may be regarded as themselves the offspring of steam-power. When England by the use of steam and of ever-improving engines for the utilisation of steam-power became able to produce more corn and coal, to produce and manufacture more iron, and to manufacture more cotton, and when improved communication by sea and land enabled her to get from every country in the world good prices for her immense surplus production, her sons and daughters found themselves in a position to support a family at an earlier age than their ancestors. The offspring of these earlier marriages, in spite of their numbers, were no more likely than the more limited offspring produced by earlier generations in less productive ages to die of starvation or insufficient nourishment in infancy, and when they grew up, found the means of subsistence still growing, owing to still further improvements in machinery. So they married young like their parents, and brought into the world healthy children, the usual proportion of which were able to survive.

It must not, however, be assumed that the increasing population found the struggle for existence any less severe than their ancestors. It seems unfortunately to be the truth that in England and most other countries the population is always much more than is warranted by the productive powers of land and labour. Whether those productive powers be great or small, increasing or stationary, large fractions of every people seem to be condemned to suffer the miseries of starvation. Of course, if the rich were to abstain from their consumption of expensive luxuries, there would be enough for all for a time. But even this remedy would be only temporary, and would, in a generation, be extinguished by increase of population. As this forbearance on the part of the rich is practically out of the question, in estimating whether the population exceeds the productive powers or not we must assume that a large amount of production will be wasted on expensive luxury. How far the population is excessive in each nation depends not on the amount of production but on the relation between the production not wasted in luxury and the existing population, which is determined by the national character and the standard of comfort in the mind of the average man. A people living in a poor barren country may enjoy a high average of comfort, and have a small percentage of pauperism, if they are prudent enough not to marry until they have the means of supporting a family. No particular age can be fixed upon as the proper age for marriage from an economical point of view. In a country of rapidly-increasing wealth it may be prudent for a people to marry at an age which in other countries would mean starvation. If inventions merely increased productive power, they would necessarily increase comfort and diminish starvation. But unfortunately the effect of invention does not stop short at increase of production. Directly by inventive discovery an increase of wealth takes place, the national soul seems to cry out, " Let us increase and multiply." Thus it is that the saying of Christ, that the poor we will always have, has been confirmed by unvarying experience up to the present day as a political, economical generalization without exception.

Yet, but for the facts of past history, it might seem not impossible that poverty might have been exterminated by increase of productive power. If since the year 1800 the population of England had remained stationary at 8,500,000, or, if some great plague or war were suddenly to reduce the population of the country to that limit, then we should have now the same number of men as then lived in England, but by modern mechanical science they would be able to extract far more wealth out of land and sea than the men of 1800. Thus the average of wealth would be so much higher that there would be abundance for everybody, and starvation and even poverty would be unknown through the length and breadth of the land. But no preacher of prudence arose with sufficient foresight and power of eloquence to persuade the nation to seize the golden opportunity presented them and better their average position. So they did not realise the fact that progress in inventive mechanical skill will never banish want and famine, unless it be accompanied by increased prudence and a higher standard of comfort. Whether with these accompaniments it might increase the general happiness we shall have afterwards to consider. So far as the history of the past has gone, it does not appear that any mechanical invention has permanently increased general happiness by rendering the struggle for existence less severe. Temporary good effects in that direction such inventions may have had. If rotation of crops is suddenly introduced into an agricultural country where this system was previously unknown, the increased production will precede for a shorter or longer time the rise of population. However quickly men and women begin to marry on the strength of the increased wealth in the country, it will be some time before enough new mouths appear to swallow up the increase. During this short interval life will be easier, and there will be less of the pains of starvation and poverty. Thus, according to Mr. Leone Levi's calculations, in the actively inventive period between 1857 and 1884, the average money wages of working men in the United Kingdom rose about 42 per cent. During the interval the purchasing power of money was, at any rate, not diminished. If rent, meat, butter and cheese are dearer, tea, sugar, rice, and bread are cheaper ; so that the average working man would appear to be really better off now than he was thirty years ago. It is clear that, if these calculations are correct, the rapid increase of population has of late years not quite kept pace with the more rapid increase of production. Let it not be supposed that this is a contradictory instance to the principles of Malthus. The improvement is evidently due partly to the relief from the pressure of population afforded by emigration, and still more to increased prudence among the working classes which is evidenced by the later average of the age of marriage. Men and women have been gradually learning the advisability of postponing marriage until they have saved something on which to support a family, and now in England and Wales bachelors marry at the comparatively late mean age of 26·2 and spinsters at 24·6 years.

This change is probably due to the influence of education, which may also affect population by making men and women think of the future, and also in another way, if, as seems to be the case, intellectual development is prejudicial to reproductive power. But all this temporary improvement of the condition of the working classes is not very much to boast of. After all we have not yet arrived at a condition of universal material well-being, and, in spite of all the mechanical inventions that have been made in the nineteenth century, English labourers are probably not as well off as they were at a far earlier stage of productive progress when England could only support about 5,000,000 inhabitants. In the days of Henry VIII., as we read in Froude's history, the artizan was better off than the agricultural labourer, and the agricultural labourer received, "steadily and regularly if well conducted, an equivalent of something near to twenty shillings a week, the wages at present paid in English colonies," and had in addition land in connexion with his house and generally the right to gather fuel from a neighbouring common and use it as pasture for his live stock. Each agricultural labourer now earns in wages, in spite of all the improvements in agricultural machinery, from ten to eighteen shillings a week, and is generally out of work for part of the year.

We must next consider the third of Bacon's three favourite types of prolific invention, the art of printing. Any claims that it may have to the promotion of happiness by spreading knowledge we have already considered implicitly in considering whether knowledge of itself adds to happiness. So far as the art of printing has by communicating from one country to another the discoveries of the nations which stand intellectually in the forefront of the world, it is only one of the many means towards the increase of population, and is to be accepted or rejected according as we are optimists or pessimists. But it has had other effects, which require separate con-

sideration. Literature has been immensely extended by
the art of printing, and the reading of literary works is
a direct source of pleasure. A literary man of ordinary
means in the present day has, owing to the invention of
printing, far more books on his shelves than were possessed
by Solomon, Socrates, or King Alfred. He can buy
Shakespeare for sixpence, the whole Bible for a shilling,
and without much heavier outlay can provide himself
with the masterpieces of foreign literature. What an
immense addition it would seem to be to the happiness
of the world that even the poorer classes have abundant
opportunities of spending their hours of leisure in reading Scott, Dickens, Shakespeare, and Milton ! Surely all
this is clear gain. The sum of the happiness enjoyed in
the reading of good books is very large, is not gained at
the expense of others, and is not necessarily preceded by
the pains of desire or followed by the pains of satiety.
But unfortunately it is not only good books that are
printed. The art of printing, besides cheapening classical
works, causes the dissemination of a vast amount of
worthless and pernicious productions, which are read
more greedily than the works of great and good men.
The reading of sensational and fleshly novels wastes
valuable time, exhausts the brain, and poisons the souls
of countless readers. The very multitude of books and
newspapers produced yearly owing to the perfection of
the art of printing militates against happiness. The
natural result of the multitude of printed matter put before the public is that reading is rapid and superficial.
Many men, who would derive much more happiness from
a careful study of Homer, Shakespeare, and Milton,
fritter away their wits in the consumption of innumer-
able novels, magazines and newspapers, and derive there-
from no solid satisfaction and no real addition to their
happiness.

It may be answered that the very fact that such
things are preferred to better literature shows that

they afford more pleasure. But this is not the case. The fact that most children would prefer to live upon sweetmeats rather than beef, mutton, or bread does not prove that they would be happier if they could carry out their wishes. Men with regard to literature are like children. They sacrifice as a rule the possibility of more permanent enjoyment to the pleasure of the moment, and the vast amount of bad literature that is printed enables them to do so more easily. Under the circumstances, as an extensive exercise of censorship of the press would be incompatible with modern ideas of liberty, it is no wonder that many sigh for the old times before the invention of printing, when children, instead of possessing beautifully printed picture books with Weatherly's verse and Kate Greenaway's illustrations, used to hearken at their nurse's knee to old national ballads about Wallace wight, doughty Douglas, and fiery Percy, and when their parents by a kindly necessity were forced to read over and over again, if they happened to have acquired the power of reading, only such works as had been deemed worthy of being copied by the slow process of writing.

If it be replied that in those old times of which we are thinking, owing to the want of printing, very few found it worth their while to learn to read, so that the pleasures of reading were unknown to the majority of the people, we may well doubt in reply whether the power of reading adds to the happiness of the average man. In fact it may fairly be said that the average man reads too much for his health and therefore for his happiness. Many a man who has to earn subsistence for his family by sedentary work indoors, spends his few hours of leisure over a fire with a newspaper or magazine in his hands, when he might be restoring his health by walking, rifle-shooting, rowing or cricket. One class, however, may be acknowledged to derive on the whole much advantage to their happiness from reading. It

c

consists of those whose work in life is muscular work in the open air, and who therefore may without injury to themselves seek their relaxation indoors. The soldier and the agricultural labourer must find the power of reading a real direct source of pleasure, and it need not indirectly hurt their happiness by undermining their health. But against the happiness that the power of reading confers on the soldier and the sailor, and those who from weakness of body or peculiar mental disposition are unable to enjoy out-door pleasure, must be weighed the ill effects of excessive study on a large fraction of each of those nations whom the art of printing has rendered learned. How many Germans, Frenchmen and Englishmen have had their health and happiness utterly ruined by poring over printed books. In England the baneful effects of over-study sometimes become perceptible before the child has left the nursery. Competitive examinations for scholarships are held by our chief public schools for very young boys at the age when they come up for their entrance examination. This practice entails hard cramming of promising boys even in preparatory schools. Every public school in its anxiety to get the first pick of the boys prepared at preparatory schools naturally makes the scholarship age lower and lower, and thus there is a tendency for the competition and cramming to commence from an earlier and yet earlier age. This system of over-study continues in the case of boys likely to win scholarships or pass hard examinations through the years of growth, when a boy ought to be laying up stores of physical strength ; and at an earlier or later stage many break down with ruined health and exhausted spirits, miserable beings to whom life in the future can afford little joy.

Having thus seen that the happiness due to the invention of printing is so inextricably combined with a large amount of misery due to the same cause, that it is impossible to see clearly whether the happiness or the pain predominates, we may now proceed to consider the material comforts conferred upon the world by inventive activity. Certainly they have greatly increased in number, especially during the last hundred years, but that this increase has really added to the happiness of the world is by no means equally certain. The modern has such a much greater abundance of these comforts than the ancient that on a superficial view he would seem to be necessarily far happier. How many luxuries and conveniences are enjoyed by the London clerk that were denied to Alcibiades, and Crassus, and Thomas Beckett. Let us verify this by accompanying a London clerk through an ordinary day of his life. He comes down to his breakfast-room, the floor of which is spread with a Kidderminster carpet, while the state apartments of Thomas Beckett were strewn with clean hay or straw in winter and green boughs and rushes in summer. A fire of coal, first used in England in 1280, is burning in a well-made fireplace, and the smoke is conducted out by a chimney, whereas in the early middle ages it would have burnt in a hole in the middle of the room with an opening in the centre of the roof to emit such part of the smoke as might choose to go straight upward. And then what a comfortable, nay, comparatively speaking, luxurious breakfast does he sit down to ! He puts a lump or two of sugar, first introduced into Europe by the Venetians and Genoese in the fourteenth and fifteenth century, or perhaps, if sugar does not agree with his health, he puts a tabloid of the recently-discovered substance called saccharine into a cup of snow-white porcelain such as was first imported into Europe from China and Japan in 1518, and first manufactured in England at Chelsea in 1702. He then helps himself to tea, which was in this country in the days of Pepys [1] a novelty and an expensive luxury, or cocoa which was

[1] "I sent for a cup of tea (a Chinese drink), of which I had never drank before." "Pepys' Diary," Sept. 25th, 1661.

first brought from Mexico in the beginning of the six-
teenth century. Beside his plate, which is also of porcelain, is that convenient instrument a fork, which was
introduced into England from Italy in the reign of
James I. If not solid silver, it has been overlaid with
silver through the agency of electricity. His breakfast
dish may be home-made bacon or perhaps salmon that
has come all the way from Labrador, or 'meat flavoured
with Indian curry powder. But it would be tedious to
follow him in the omnibus or underground railway to his
desk and back again to his dinner at night. Let us
rather content ourselves with enumerating a few of the
modern appliances by which the course of his life is
made smooth and pleasant. Among them will be baro-
meters, thermometers, gas, clocks, watches, steel pens,
artificial ice, coffee, potatoes, tobacco, pianos, photo-
graphs, postage stamps, post-cards, money orders, banks,
pins, needles, bicycles, tricycles, argand lamps, lightning
conductors, matches, umbrellas. All these and much
else resulting from modern discoveries, the civilised man
of the middle-class now enjoys, and, if he were deprived
of them and compelled to live with no other comforts but
those enjoyed by Alcibiades, Crassus, and Thomas Beckett,
he would bemoan himself with much the same feelings
as Ovid experienced when he was banished from Imperial
Rome to barbarous Tomi.

Yet it does not follow that he is any happier than the
average member of the middle class was in past centuries.
All these wonderful inventions, which would sound like
fairy tales rather than sober truth to ancient Greek, or
early Englishmen, are to the man of the nineteenth century matters of course. We know well enough that we
do not enjoy our breakfasts of viands collected from the
four corners of the earth a bit more than Queen Eliza-
beth, who had to prepare herself for the labours of the
day with a solid foundation of English beef, English ale,
and English bread. When a shower of rain falls, it is a

great comfort to have an umbrella to keep the drops off
our face and the upper parts of our body; but the constant use of umbrellas has made us so effeminately sensi-
tive to wet that with our umbrellas up we suffer more
from the rain that wets our trousers than our ancestors
did when a shower of rain fell all over their hats, face,
and clothes, or, to go further back, than our still more
distant ancestors suffered when the rain fell on the
painted skin of their unclothed bodies. It is very convenient for the Englishman in India to be able to apprise
his friends in England by telegram that he is at the
point of death, but, if the telegraph had never been invented, he would never have dreamt of the possibility of
so doing and would not have felt any pain at having to
keep his friends waiting three weeks longer for the news.
It is considered a great blessing by the travelling Englishman that he is able to get to and from India
in journeys of less than three weeks; but, if loco-
motives and steamships had never been invented, instead
of spending the winter in India he would have con-
tentedly and with equal satisfaction to himself have gone
to winter in the south of France, the south of Devon-
shire, or have stopped at home. Our desires are, unfortunately, quite able to keep pace with the means of
satisfying them; so that now, while our grandparents
managed to get quite well through life with little or no
change of air and scene, we think, and are supported in
the idea by our medical advisers, that we must for the
benefit of our health occasionally take rushes to Switzerland, Italy, Australia, America or more remote quarters
of the world; and, if we have not the money to pay the
expense, we remain at home, while our friends are wandering abroad, and, owing to our forced inaction, feel
much the same feelings as an active dog must feel in his
chain. The merchant of to-day, if he cannot get a train
to carry him at the rate of forty miles an hour to his
family at the sea side, suffers as much annoyance as the

traveller in coaching days felt when his coach did not go
at whatever happened to be in his day the average rate
of mail coaches. The pleasure derived from such sources
depends entirely on custom and comparison. The most
ingeniously devised contrivance, if possessed by everybody, gives no more pleasure to the possessor than air or
water, although, as is also the case with air and water,
the deprivation of them may cause great pain. If dia-
monds were as common as daisies, the possession of a
diamond would afford no more pleasure than the possession of a daisy. At least this is surely the case with all
the complicated machinery of modern luxury. Whether
the same can be said of medical contrivances for curing
disease and alleviating pain must be considered in the
following chapter.

In considering the effects of mechanical inventions
some thinkers are inclined so far to depart from the
opinion of the majority as to condemn them as entirely
destructive of happiness. The most eloquent exponent
of this view is Mr. Ruskin.[1]   I have myself heard him at
those charming breakfast parties in his Oxford rooms, at
which he gathered round his table his fellow labourers at
the Hinksey Road, anticipate half in jest, half in earnest,
the day when his disciples would pull down the railway
embankments which he thinks so ugly and convert them
into strawberry beds. All through his works we find
continual complaints of the ugliness of the factories and
railway stations and other results of modern mechanical
inventions, and regret for the old times when men walked
on their feet and rode horses instead of driving steam
engines or being shut up in railway carriages. There is
no reason why a utilitarian should not adopt this view.
It is possible for the philosophical utilitarian to be
utterly opposed to what are popularly but wrongly
called utilitarian ideas. The true utilitarian may reasonably prefer parks and picture galleries to factories and

[1] See especially *Fors Clavigera*, Letter XLIV.

railway stations, and may without inconsistency oppose the tendency of modern invention which is driving the human race to earn their living as the workers of complicated iron machines instead of leading the open-air life of their ancestors. Only he must clearly convince himself that the change is diminishing the average happiness. At first sight one is inclined to think that it is having this effect. Modern invention, especially the invention of steam power, condemns ever-increasing numbers of the human race to work in the grimy darkness of mines or amid the clanging machinery of a great factory. They live in crowded towns, the ground of which is black with coal dust, while the heaven is obscured by smoke. How easy to contrast this with the open-air life of the agriculturist or the hunter among all the beauties of nature.

But after all it is doubtful whether the agricultural life is any happier than that lived by factory hands. The ideas of the agricultural life formed by literary men are rather those of casual observers than of the workers themselves. The cultured man wearied with hard work in great cities enjoys a ramble through the country or a little gardening amongst the flowers of his pleasure grounds, but he should not therefore suppose that the same feelings are felt by the ditcher working all the long day in a marshy meadow with the mud rising almost to his knees. *O fortunati nimium sua si bona norint Agricolæ!* But they do not know their own blessings, and therefore they are not too happy. They are not mentally capable as a rule of enjoying all the pleasures that the literary man who envies their lot derives from the scenery of forest, hill, and valley. They prefer life in the slums of a great city to rural Arcadias, and their preference should not be disregarded as the ignorant opinion of men who do not know what is good for them. Unless we have reason to the contrary, we may suppose that men know themselves best what makes for their own

happiness. Therefore the fact that so many agricultur-
ists leave their country life to work in city factories, and
that so few care to return to their rural life must be
given due weight. Also it must be admitted that minds
of a healthy temperament may derive pleasure and eleva-
tion of mind even from the associations of a life among
machinery. The poet of American democracy can include among his joys of life the driving of a locomotive,
" the engineer's joys ! to go with a locomotive ! to hear
the hiss of steam, the merry shriek, the steam whistle,
the laughing locomotive ! to push with resistless way and
speed off in the distance," and even the miner's joys " to
work in mines, or forging iron, foundry casting, the
foundry itself, the rude high roof, the ample and
shadowed space, the furnace, the hot liquid pour'd out
and running." On the other hand, the reverse of the
Utopian pictures of agricultural life usually given in
literature may be seen in such works as *A Village
Tragedy* and *The History of an African Farm.*

Such considerations must prevent us from feeling confident that an agricultural labourer's life is less miserable
than that of a factory hand. On the other hand, we can
scarcely think it more miserable. For it is impossible to
read the accounts given of the life of the very poor in great
cities, and to see their pale, haggard faces in the streets,
and yet suppose that the average happiness has been
really increased by the crowding into great manufacturing cities that has resulted from the development of
mechanical art. We should rather leave the question
open, and, not knowing whether man is happier or
unhappier labouring in a factory than he would be
labouring in the field, act as if the invention of steam
power had neither improved nor diminished the average
happiness of the labourer's life.

CHAPTER IV.

IN discussing the felicific effects of the discoveries of medical science we may begin by assuming that good health is a source of happiness, and bad health of unhappiness. The assumption will hardly be disputed. A healthy man is *pro tanto* happier than an unhealthy one, a healthy nation than an unhealthy nation, a healthy generation than an unhealthy generation. This leads us to the consideration of a large number of inventions intended to benefit health, and of a body of professional men who always consider themselves, and are generally considered by others to be in a peculiar way the promoters of the happiness of the human race. It must be admitted not only that health promotes happiness, but also that medical men often by their prescriptions free us from pain and restore us to health. He would be a rash man who in the present day would dispute the fact that quinine exerts a beneficial tendency against fever, that vaccination often saves the person vaccinated from small-pox, and that chloroform administered during surgical operations saves the patient from intense pain. This being granted, it would seem to follow that doctors in the exercise of their profession, by discovering and administering cures, increase the happiness and diminish the misery of the human race.

But the argument is at any rate to a great extent fallacious. Medical science can improve the health of the individual; but it does not necessarily follow that it can improve the health of the race. This can be most clearly seen by the consideration of the effects of the

progress made in midwifery.   Why is it that savage
women are without assistance delivered as easily or
more easily than civilised women with all the appliances
of medical science ?   The reason is that the savage
women being the descendants of many generations of
mothers, all of whom have been able to bear children
without assistance from art, have inherited that capability.   Savage women, who do not happen to be able
to do so, die off and leave no descendants.   In civilised
countries, on the contrary, women who would without
medical help have no children are enabled to do so, and
their children are likely to resemble their mothers when
their time comes to be mothers.   Yet there is no doubt
this branch of the medical art benefits the individual.
It saves many an individual mother from broken health
and early death, even though it may do so at the expense
of the general happiness.   Or perhaps we should rather
say "without promoting the general happiness."   For it is
very possible that the civilised woman with medical help
manages to get through her troubles with about as little
suffering as the savage mother.

The fact that medical science may benefit the individual and yet not benefit the race may be proved by
many instances of nations and tribes that have flourished
in health and strength with no help from medicine or in
spite of the popularity of cures that must have harmed
the individual.   The Tuaric, an African tribe, is an
instance of this, stretching from ancient times to the
present day.   Herodotus (IV. 187) says that the
healthiest men he knew were the Libyans, and that
their secret of health was the burning of the veins of
their forehead.   According to Rawlinson the Tuaric have
the best claim to be regarded as the direct descendants
of the Libyans of Herodotus.   Certainly they exhibit
the same power of flourishing in spite of perverse ideas
of the conditions of good health, and they have the
same fondness for cautery as a cure.   Captain Lyon, who

visited them in the beginning of the century, found that they burnt with a hot iron those afflicted with liver complaint, enlargement of spleen, asthma, consumption, rupture and stricture. Blind men had their temples burned, and pieces of onion placed between their eyes. This people had the most decided aversion to washing. " God," they said, " never intended that man should injure his health, if he could avoid it ; water having been given to man to drink and cook with, it does not agree with the skin of a Tuaric who always falls sick after much washing." Yet, in spite of this and in spite of the fact that they lived in a temperature that rose to 133 degrees, Captain Lyon described them as being " the finest race of men he ever saw, tall, straight, and handsome."

The same conclusion, that medical skill helps the individual without helping the race, may be arrived at by a comparison between modern and ancient times. There is no doubt, that modern medical skill often lengthens the life of a sick man, and enables him to live to old age, when, without the doctor's aid or with only such aid as he could have got in ancient times or in the middle ages, he would have died in youth or early manhood. Yet there is every reason to believe that the average of human life is no higher now than it was in the days of ancient Greece and Rome and in the middle ages. Unfortunately, it is only possible to get very fragmentary statistics of the duration of life in ancient times. But it is better methodically to use such fragmentary statistics, than for any one to quote carefully selected instances of longevity or early death to support the view he himself wishes to uphold. It might be interesting and amusing, to consider whether Masinissa at the age of 88 charging at the head of his cavalry, was a more remarkable instance of longevity than the grandfather of the present German Emperor, or whether Sophocles in his old age outdid the poetical work of the old age of Tennyson and Browning, or whether any ancient orator could rival the feats performed by Mr. Gladstone in the eighth decade of his life. But such bandying of individual instances would be futile as a means of arriving at a probable conclusion. We are much more likely to effect our object, if we use a fair number of instances collected by some one else who was not thinking of the question of longevity, and see what conclusions they point to. Such an opportunity is afforded us by the editor of "Everybody's Pocket Cyclopædia," who brings together the names of one hundred and nine eminent men of ancient and modern times, and incidentally mentions the dates of their birth and death. We may accept as correct the dates there given, and remove out of consideration nine famous men whose ages are either not given in the list, viz., Homer, Moses, Zoroaster, Confucius, Buddha, and Pythagoras, or given conjecturally, viz., St. Paul, Hippocrates and Galen. Thus we have left one hundred eminent men, who may be divided into three classes, the first class containing twenty-two men who lived before the Christian era ; the second class, fifty-two men born in the Christian era before the commencement of the eighteenth century ; while the third class will consist of twenty-six persons born after the commencement of the eighteenth century. These examples, though necessarily limited in number, are in quality about as good as we could possibly have, as they consist of eminent men, and eminent men usually have the best available medical advice. So that statistics of eminent men are much better for the purpose of throwing light on the efficacy of medical science than statistics of ordinary men. The names of the persons in the three classes with their ages, will be found to be as follows :—

First Class.—Pindar, 79 ; Æschylus, 69 ; Sophocles, 90 ; Euripides, 74 ; Aristophanes, 64 ; Menander, 51 ; Lucretius, 40 ; Virgil, 51 ; Phidias, 59 : Praxiteles, 70 ; Socrates, 70 ; Plato, 81 ; Aristotle, 62 ; Herodotus, 78 ; Thucydides, 69 : Demosthenes, 63 ;

Cicero, 63 ; Archimedes, 75 ; Pericles, 70 ; Alexander, 33 ; Hannibal, 64 ; Cæsar, 56.

Second Class.—Dante, 60 ; Rabelais, 70 ; Cervantes, 69 ; Shakespeare, 52 ; Milton, 66 ; Moliere, 51 : Leonardo da Vinci, 67 ; Michael Angelo, 89 ; Raphael, 37 ; Correggio, 60 ; Titian, 96 ; Rubens, 63 ; Rembrandt, 62 ; Bach, 65 ; Handel, 74 ; Mahomet, 62 ; St. Augustine, 76 ; St. Bernard, 62 ; St. Francis of Assisi, 44 ; Erasmus, 70 ; Luther, 63 ; Calvin, 55 ; Loyola, 65 : Bossuet, 87 ; St. Thomas Aquinas, 47 ; Bacon, 65 : Descartes, 54 ; Spinoza, 45 ; Locke, 72 ; Leibnitz, 70 ; Berkeley, 68 ; Tacitus, 63 ; Plutarch, 70 ; Montaigne, 59 ; Montesquieu, 66 ; Voltaire, 84 ; Copernicus, 70 ; Kepler, 59 ; Galileo, 78 ; Harvey, 79 ; Newton, 85 ; Charlemagne 72 ; Alfred the Great, 52 : William the Conqueror, 60 ; Charles V., 58 ; William the Silent, 51 ; Richelieu, 57 ; Cromwell, 59 ; Peter the Great, 53 ; Guttenberg, 68 ; Columbus, 70 ; Palissy, 80.

Third Class.—Goethe, 83 ; Scott, 61 ; Mozart, 35 ; Beethoven, 58 ; J. Wesley, 88 ; Hume, 65 ; Kant, 80 ; Diderot, 71 ; Lessing, 52 ; Gibbon, 57 ; Linnæus, 71 : Lavoisier, 51 ; Bichat, 31 ; Cuvier, 63 ; Frederick, 74 ; Washington, 67 ; Jefferson, 83 ; Nelson, 47 ; Napoleon, 52 ; Wellington, 83 ; Franklin, 84 ; Montgolfier, 70 ; Howard, 64 ; Arkwright, 60 ; J. Watt, 83 ; Stephenson, 67.

Omitted from the lists owing to uncertainty of age at death.— Homer, Moses, Zoroaster, Confucius, Buddha, St. Paul, Pythagoras, Hippocrates, Galen.

Anyone who works out the sum will find that the average age of the first class is $65\frac{1}{22}$, of the second class, $64\frac{51}{52}$, and of the third class $65\frac{10}{26}$. These statistics show no clear evidence of prolongation of the average of life having been secured by the great advance made in medical science during the last two centuries. Of the lives mentioned in the list, but not included in the statistics above, Moses, as we read in the Bible, " was one hundred and twenty years old when he died," and we are given the following additional information interesting from a medical point of view that " his eye was not dim, nor his natural force abated." Hippocrates is credited in the list with a hundred and three years of life, but the editor has put a note of interrogation after the dates, so that it seems safer to leave him out of consideration. Could Hippocrates and Moses, or Hippocrates alone have been added to the first class of lives, the lives before the Christian era would have attained a decidedly higher average than either of the two subsequent periods. Galen's years are given as seventy in the cyclopædia, the dates being followed by a note of interrogation as in the case of Hippocrates. His inclusion in the second class would raise the average of the second class to over 66, while the insertion of St. Paul, who, according to the dates given in the list, lived either 62 or 55 years, would slightly reduce it.

Let us now take another comparison. We must still confine ourselves to eminent men as the ancient world gives us no statistics of the longevity of ordinary men. Statesmen will not give us a fair comparison, as those who engaged in politics in ancient days had their lives so very often shortened by constant wars, executions or political assassination. Literary men will, however, afford a fair basis of comparison, and let us this time confine ourselves to them only, taking care not to choose our instances.

In the account given in the Encyclopædia Britannica of Greek Literature down to its decadence, if we take the names of all the Greek poets and prose writers mentioned therein and look them out in Smith's biographical dictionary, we find a conjectural or unconjectural statement given of the age of twenty-eight of them. They will be found to be Solon, 80; Xenophanes over 90; Simonides of Ceos, 89; Anacreon, 85; Stesichorus, 80; Pindar, 80; Æschylus, 69; Sophocles, 90; Euripides, 75; Cratinus, 97; Eupolis, 35; Aristophanes, 64; Herodotus, 77 at least; Anaximander, 64; Hellanicus, 85; Thucydides, 70 at most; Antiphon, 69; Xenophon, over 90; Gorgias, 105 or 109; Andocides, at least 74; Lysias, 80; Isocrates, 98; Demosthenes, 63; Æschines, 75; Lycurgus, about 73; Plato, 82; Aristotle, 63; Theophrastus, 85 or 107. For the purposes of our calculation we may ascribe to Gorgias and Theophrastus the ages of 107 and 96, the means between the two extremes given in the dictionary. The average age will then be found to be considerably over 78, and this wonderfully high average would not be diminished by excluding the ages given conjecturally, as among the conjectural ages is the age of Eupolis given at 35.

Let us compare with this the literary men who happen to be mentioned in the last period of English Literature sketched in the same Encyclopædia, taking their ages from Vincent's "Dictionary of Biography," published in 1878. They are Wordsworth, 80; Coleridge, 62; Southey, 69 ; Scott, 61 ; Burke, 68 ; Shelley, 30 ; Byron, 33 ; Mary Godwin, 38 ; Senior, 74 ; Horner, 39 ; Romilly, 61 ; Ricardo, 51 ; Mill, 67 ; M'Culloch, 75 ; Lancaster, 63 ; Ball, 80 ; Harriet Martineau, 74 ; Elliott, 68 ; Moore, 73. The average age of these nineteen persons is between 61 and 62.

If it be objected that of these Shelley was drowned and Romilly committed suicide, we need only glance our eyes over the ancient list to find that it includes two suicides, Isocrates and Demosthenes, and Antiphon who was put to death.

If it be objected that the English list only reaches down to 1832, since when medical science has made brilliant and rapid progress, I reply that medical science has surely made immense strides between the days of Aristotle and the beginning of the present century, and that the comparison indicates clearly enough the inefficacy of that progress to increase average longevity. It is possible that the extraordinarily rapid advance of medical science since the beginning of this century may have temporarily increased longevity, but, for the reasons given below, this improvement can hardly be permanent. And even the death rate of eminent men during the last few years cannot rival that of the great Greek poets, historians, and orators. To support this, let us examine the obituary list given in Whitaker's Almanack for 1890.

It gives the ages at death of 238 eminent men who died in 1888-1889, and the average will be found to be a little under 70, a wonderfully high average, but far below the average taken from the literary men of ancient Greece.

Thus, on the whole, it is clear that eminent men enjoyed about as long lives in ancient as in modern times, and it is natural, in the absence of evidence to the contrary, to infer that the generalisation may be extended to the lives of ordinary men, that is, of the whole human race. The men of the ancient world and of the middle ages lived just as long as we do in the nineteenth century, and, if they lived as long, it is natural to suppose that they enjoyed just as good health. So that medical science seems to have done nothing to improve the health or lengthen the life of the human race as a whole. Had it done so, it would have promoted happiness. For health promotes happiness, and short lives and frequent deaths involve much painful mourning among bereft relations and friends.

If it be asked how medical science can improve the health of the individual without improving the health of the race, the answer is not far to seek. In fact the explanation has been given above in considering the obstetric branch of medical science. We have only to apply more generally the explanation there given. A hint towards the solution may be found in the Republic of Plato, who praises Asclepius because "bodies, which disease had penetrated through and through, he would not have attempted to cure by gradual process of evacuation and infusion ; he did not want to lengthen out useless lives, or that weak fathers should beget weaker sons; if a man was not able to live in the ordinary way he had no business to cure him, for he would have done no good either to the man himself or to the state." Medical science, if its operation could be strictly limited according to the lines laid down by Plato, would increase the average health and happiness. There are cases in which a sick man after his cure is likely to enjoy more than the average health. If an exceptionally healthy man is saved from dying of cholera, he may be as healthy after his cure as he was before he was ill, and the saving of such a life is a gain to the average health and happiness. In other cases a man who is below the average health may, by medical skill, be improved in health so much as to enjoy more than the average health. It is not, however, to be expected that either by legal enactment or public opinion doctors will ever be compelled to confine their ministrations to those whom they have a fair chance of raising above the average health. But until such restrictions are laid upon doctors, medical science cannot be admitted to be a constant element in the diminution of the sum of human pain. Medical science, as long as it cures without discrimination all who can pay their doctor's bills or get attendance for nothing, does good to the general health by giving good health to the moderately healthy, but it cancels its good work by enabling those, who would otherwise die, to live on in bad health, and in some cases produce offspring inheriting their weakness and transmitting it to a third generation.

And it must be remembered that the mere prevention of the death of individuals, unless it leads to a rise in the average health and length of life, is a doubtful benefit to the general happiness. Every life saved by a doctor may be expected to diminish the sum of misery by saving his relations and friends from the grief of bereavement. But on the other hand, as there is only a limited amount of subsistence in the earth at a given time, every death leaves more to be divided among those who do not die. And the saving of lives makes the struggle for existence harder than it would otherwise be. The death of the breadwinner of a family leaves his wife and children destitute, but may enable some other father of a family who succeeds to his vacant post to support his family, which would otherwise have suffered from want. On these

D

grounds the mere saving of life, unless it improves the average health and length of life, is a doubtful benefit to the world, and every doctor should realise the fact that, by enabling a dying man to live, he probably somewhere in the world causes a living man to die, and so benefits the payer of his fee at the expense of some unknown person. Let him therefore abstain from supposing himself a benefactor of the human race on the score of all such triumphs of his art. The medical man who in the exercise of his profession saves lives, by so doing sometimes increases and sometimes decreases the general happiness. He generally increases it when the person saved lives on in more than average health, and generally decreases it when the person saved is so weakened by the disease of which he is cured that his health is below the average.

But some will oppose this reasoning and these statistics by other statistics which seem to point in the opposite direction, and to show that the saving of lives by modern medical science is proved by the increased length of life to have improved the average health. It is popularly believed that the death rate in the nineteenth century is far lower than it ever was before, and this belief is supported by appeals to statistics. We read in " Chambers' Information for the People," that " in England during the period 1690-1820 the ratio of deaths to the population fell no less than two fifths." This statement so confidently put forward cannot rest on any sure foundation. Mr. N. A. Humphreys, in the " Statistical Journal " for June, 1883, remarks that "It is scarcely necessary to say that very little is known of the variations in the annual death-rate in England prior to the establishment of civil registration in 1837. The Registrar-General's mortality statistics embrace the forty-five years, 1838-1882, and constitute the only trustworthy basis for calculations as to the duration of life in England." The conclusion arrived at in " Chambers' Information for the People " must depend partly on London Bills of Mortality, and

partly on the experience of insurance companies, etc. The
evidence of the former source of information cannot be
applied without danger to the whole of England. It is
quite possible that sanitary improvements might temporarily improve the death-rate of great cities without
affecting the rural districts. In fact, this is a difference
that we should naturally expect even without the guidance of statistics. In the country there is less room for
sanitary improvement. The death-rate in great cities
may partly be attributed to rural immigrants unaccus-
tomed to the sanitary or unsanitary conditions of life in
great cities. This part of the city death-rate will be
lessened by sanitary improvement, and at the same time
the old civic population, as their families have been long
settled in the city, the sanitary condition of which has been
improved, being descended from ancestors well weeded by
much more trying sanitary circumstances, will die less
plentifully until their average power of resisting disease
has been weakened by the less stringent natural selection
due to improved sanitation. These considerations show
that the health of great cities may improve without a
corresponding improvement in the country generally. And
this conclusion is verified by the returns of the Registrar-
General for the current decade, which are as follows :—

	1881-1886.	1887.	1888.
Urban Districts,	20·3	19·7	18·4
Rural Districts,	17·6	17·2	16·7

These figures show that the late improvement in health
has been about twice as great in cities as in the country.

Further, owing to the practice of selection, the experience of insurance companies is not by any means to be
relied upon. The advance of medical science enables the
medical advisers of companies more unerringly every
year to reject bad lives. It is probable that when insurance companies were first started they rejected fewer lives,

and it is certain that the conditions of longevity being then less known the rejections were made with less skill. So that the improvement in assured lives cannot be expected to be true of the whole population. Nevertheless, although the consultation of mortality tables and of the records of insurance companies has undoubtedly given an exaggerated view of the improvement in health before 1838, there is still room to believe that there was a very distinct progress made in this respect between the end of the seventeenth century and the beginning of the nineteenth.

But is this progress, if it may safely without reliable statistics be assumed to have taken place, due to sanitation and medical science or to some more potent cause? In the middle of the seventeenth century the English nation began to drink spirits on a large scale, and so introduced into their midst a terrible engine of destruction. From 1691 to 1708 the annual consumption of home made spirits on which duty was paid rose from 539,868 to 1,155,063 gallons, and in 1735 it had reached 6,440,454 gallons. The sudden introduction of this deadly plague must have made the death-rate abnormally high at the end of the seventeenth century, and the rapidly increasing popularity of the poison until 1735, the year of the gin bill, must have kept it high. But as time went on, like all other plagues it began to work its own cure. Most of the Englishmen living in the beginning of the nineteenth century were descendants of two or three generations who had managed to drink spirits and live and have children. Though they still went on drinking about as much spirits as their ancestors, the process of natural selection that had been going on before they were born enabled them to bear it better. Thus, at the beginning of this century, England was only struggling back by the action of natural selection to the normal death-rate which had been temporarily suspended by the drinking of spirits. No one pretends that the death-rate is absolutely fixed. What appears to be the truth is that it swings back and forward on either side of the mean death-rate with the oscillatory movement of a pendulum. Having been violently disturbed by the introduction of the practice of drinking spirits in the end of the seventeenth century, it began to approach the mean again in the beginning of the nineteenth, and remained there for some time.

Mr. Humphreys points out in the article already quoted that, " although the death-rate varied from year to year, it may be said to have remained practically stationary during the thirty years 1838-70." Since then there has however been a marked improvement. The mean death-rate for England from 1871 to 1880 was 21·5, and from 1881-1888 it was 19·2, the best two years recorded being 18·8 for 1887 and 17·8 for 1888. This improvement may be attributed to sanitary improvements, especially to the improved sanitation in great cities in which the decrease of the death-rate has been most conspicuous, but, unless the improvement in sanitation goes on for ever at the same rate as in this decade, the death-rate is likely first to cease to improve and then to move in a retrograde direction, as the average human being becomes weakened by those who are from a health point of view unfit being helped to survive. But sanitation cannot be expected to go on improving for ever. Immediately it ceases to improve, the death-rate will tend to rise. For if the sanitary condition in England, after improving steadily year by year up to the year x, after that year ceases to improve, and is the same in the year $x + 1$ as it was in the year x, a larger proportion may expect to die in the latter than in the former year, because those living in the former year will have been better weeded by themselves and their ancestors having lived in years all of which had been inferior from a sanitary point of view, while those living in the latter year will have missed, at least for the immediately preceding year, the advantage of a more stringent natural selection than they will be exposed to in the year x + 1.

There is, however, a particular class of medical discoveries to which the above disparaging reasoning does not apply, because their chief claim to value is not so much that they promote the health of individuals and prolong their lives, though they may effect this also, but that they directly diminish or annihilate pain. Anæsthetics thus stand on quite a different footing from merely curative drugs, and require separate consideration to see whether they promote general happiness. When a man suffering from great pain escapes that pain by taking chloroform, the diminution of his misery is not gained at the expense of any other being. Nor is there any reason why the anæsthetic which drives away pain in his case should in other cases be productive of pain. So far as anæsthetics are instrumental in the prolonging of individual lives and restoring health to individuals, they are no more productive of happiness than any other remedies, but in so far as they simply banish pain they are a clear addition to the happiness of the human race. Thus the inventors of anæsthetics may be regarded as men who have increased the happiness of the human race, unless the anæsthetic produces after effects of a more painful character than the pain escaped. All that can be said on the other side is that some people by the excessive use of anæsthetics ruin their health and shorten their lives. This is as true, though in a less degree, of anæsthetics, as it is of alcohol. Yet, if it has been proved satisfactorily that vaccination, quinine and all the other cures and preventives of disease that have ever been invented have had no appreciable effect in improving the health of the human race, it follows that the use of drugs productive of disease, however ruinous to the individual, cannot permanently decrease the general health and happiness. Although, like alcohol, at their first introduction they may increase the death-rate, as time goes on, and those who have not strength of mind to avoid them, or are not healthy enough to use them with impunity, die out by the process of natural selection, these drugs will not affect the death-rate any more than the excessive cold of Norway, or the excessive heat of Central Africa. So that the direct good effect of anæsthetics in preventing pain, does not seem really to be counterbalanced by any general permanent bad effects on the health and happiness of the human race.

The consideration of anæsthetics naturally suggests the advisability of euthanasia as a means for the increase of happiness. The term euthanasia has been used in two senses, in both of which it deserves to have its felicific effects estimated. Bacon in the "Advancement of Learning" recommends euthanasia, and means by the word the diminution or extinction of the pains of dying. "I esteem it," he writes, "the office of a physician not only to restore health, but to mitigate pain and dolors, and not only when such mitigation may conduce to recovery, but when it may serve to make a fair and easy passage: for it is no small felicity which Augustus Cæsar was wont to wish to himself that same euthanasia, and which was especially noted in the death of Antoninus Pius, whose death was after the fashion and semblance of a kindly and pleasant sleep. So it is written of Epicurus, that, after his disease was judged desperate, he drowned his stomach and senses with a large draught and ingurgitation of wine; whereupon the epigram was made:—

Hinc Stygias ebrius hausit aquas:

he was not sober enough to taste any bitterness of the Stygian water. But the physicians contrariwise, do make a kind of scruple and religion to stay with the patient after the disease is deplored; whereas, in my judgment, they ought both to inquire the skill, and to give the attendances for the facilitating and assuag-

ing of the pains and agonies of death." Certainly
euthanasia in this sense is in every way desirable from
a utilitarian point of view. So far as the members of
the medical faculty have by anæsthetics or other means
succeeded in diminishing the pains of death, they have
made a clear addition to the happiness of the human race.
It is only when the extinction of pain enables those who
would otherwise have died to live on in bad health that
its felicific effects become doubtful.

But some have gone farther than Bacon and recommended under the name of euthanasia not merely
diminution of the pains of death but painless extinction
of life in the case of painful and incurable disease. They
have ventured to argue that, when a man is so overcome
by the pains of an incurable disease that his life is a source
of continual pain to himself and others, it would be better
for happiness that he should be painlessly put out of misery.
No doubt it would be better for the individual sufferer,
and, if he could be painlessly killed by other than human
agency, his gain would diminish the happiness of no one
else, and would therefore be an addition to the happiness of
the world. But it is a very different matter to recommend
that such a person should be killed painlessly by his
doctor after consultation with his nearest relatives.
While there is life there is hope. How often have
doctors given up as incurable the case of a patient who
has nevertheless eventually recovered ! Much would be
added to the misery of the sick if they were continually
in fear of having their dear lives taken away without
their consent. But worst of all would be the mutual
suspicion engendered by such a course between the
nearest relations, and between the patient and his
physicians and nurses. Such evils would certainly not
be less than the bodily pain from which the individual
sufferer would be saved by accelerating the hour of his
death.

CHAPTER V.

HAVING found that medical science by interfering with the natural struggle for existence, and enabling those to live and have children, who would without its assistance have died childless at an early age, counteracts the good it would otherwise, by giving good health to those who were slightly unhealthy, have done to the race, we naturally proceed to consider the opposite extreme, which will be found in infanticide and other customs by which man has deliberately set about the task of assisting nature in weeding out the weaker, unhealthier specimens of the human type.

Would it promote the happiness of the world to simply add to the number of destructive agencies in the world, say by abolishing vaccination in order to allow small-pox to rage uncontrolled, or by promoting famine, or by advocating that men should expose themselves more to damp and cold by forswearing houses and clothes ?

In answer to this question, a distinction must be made between two classes of diseases. Some permanently weaken even those who recover from them. Therefore, the utilitarian would immediately dismiss the idea of promoting those diseases, as they would obviously not only kill the weak, but also weaken the strong. But there may be, and are certain diseases which kill the weak, and leave no effects of an evil character upon those who are strong enough to recover from them. Thus, while recovery from a sore throat leaves behind it increased liability to the same attack, which liability may doubtless be transmitted to descendants, quite the opposite is the case with small-pox and some other diseases. Small-pox, as a rule, when it fails to kill, leaves no evil effects behind. The person who has recovered is no weaker, and is indeed fortified against small-pox in the future, and probably transmits a tendency to similar immunity. In this way the prevalence of small-pox in one generation increases the health of the next generation, which will be composed of a large number of children of parents either not liable to small-pox, or strong enough to recover from it. From these considerations, it would appear that small-pox may be good for the health of the next generation. But as this advantage is gained at the expense of a large amount of disease and death in the present generation, the advantage of the future is obtained at the expense of the present, and not improbably the plus and minus quantities would be found just about to cancel each other.

Is there then no means by which this advantage to future generations may be secured without the present generation suffering from disease, and without the mourning occasioned by grief for the untimely death of human beings in the hearts of the bereaved? Several peoples have tried to improve their condition by weeding out their weaker members, but none of them have quite succeeded in effecting this in accordance with utilitarian principles. The remedy has generally been found to be as bad as, if not worse than, the evils intended to be cured. The most common form which the effort has taken is infanticide, which was commonly practised by the ancient Greeks, and, until quite recently, by the natives of India. This method of eliminating the weak is in three ways preferable to the elimination by means of disease. Infanticide is more thorough. It kills outright all those who are condemned, whereas many diseases inflicting pains equal to those of death, instead of killing leave the victim alive, but weak, to suffer the pains of ill-health for many years. Secondly, infanticide does not inflict so much pain as disease, inasmuch as infants can be quickly killed without suffering much bodily pain, and are entirely free from the mental pains of anticipated death. Thirdly, infanticide makes a better selection than disease. Though disease more often attacks and kills the weak than the strong, there are many cases in which strong men and women are carried off by disease when the weak escape. Such exceptions may also have happened in the case of infanticide, but much more rarely. Occasionally an unhealthy-looking infant may grow up into a healthy man, and a healthy infant may become an unhealthy man. But such unexpected developments certainly happen in a much smaller proportion of cases than the exceptions to the rule that disease attacks and kills the weaker and spares the stronger.

But these three advantages, though they must make infanticide really improve the health of the people among whom it is practised, are counterbalanced by the one great disadvantage that it is carried out by human agency and by the will of the parents of the child. The diminution of happiness due to the violation of the sacredness of human life, and to the dissolution of the ties of parental affection must be at least as great as the increase of happiness due to the improvement of the average health really secured by infanticide. Among the Spartans an attempt was made to supplement infanticide. Newborn infants were bathed in wine, which was supposed to strengthen the strong and kill the weak. Although no one will now believe that a wine bath could have been so doubly efficacious, the plan is interesting as an attempt to secure an ideally perfect elimination of weaker individuals.

Other peoples are said to have practised the opposite of infanticide and to have killed their old men and women. Thus, according to Strabo, the Derbices killed and ate all who passed the age of seventy, and the Caspians killed but did not eat those who had passed the same age. No doubt senicide, like infanticide, was due to rough utilitarian calculations such as could be made by barbarian intellects. It was argued that, food being scarce, it was better for the tribe to get rid of their older members, who could not do much work. It was doubtless also a point in favour of the practice that old men were really incapable of enjoying life like young men. Therefore it was deemed expedient to despatch them, and the Derbices went to a farther length in brutal utilitarianism by making the dead bodies of the old men add to their stock of food. Similar to senicide was the custom followed by the Massagetæ (Herodotus i. 216) and the Indian Padæans of killing those who were ill. Of the Padæans we read in Herodotus that "If one of their number be ill, man or woman, they take the sick person, and if he be a man the men of his acquaintance proceed to put him to death, because they say his flesh would be spoilt for them if he pined and wasted away with sickness. The man protests he is not ill in the least; but his friends will not accept his denial—in spite of all he can say they kill him and feast themselves on his body. So also if a woman be sick the women who are her friends take her and do with her exactly the same as the men." (Rawlinson's Herodotus iii. 99.) The humorous account of Herodotus illustrates how naturally, when once the sacredness of human life is forgotten, interested motives lead to killing beyond the bounds originally laid down. At first we may suppose that only those incurably ill were killed, but unscrupulous persons in time of want would stretch the regulation in a way which they thought would conduce to the general good, by killing those afflicted even with slight indisposition. A society among whom such regulations existed would at least have the advantage of escaping from the annoyance caused to his friends and relations by a hypochondriac's affectation of illness, which is so often an excuse for idleness and ill temper. No Padæan would venture to impose upon the sympathies of his friends by playing the part of a *malade imaginaire.*

Sometimes in the struggle for existence, whole peoples are eliminated by pestilence or by war, and give place to other peoples. The most conspicuous instance of this is the disappearance or decrease of the natives of Australia and America on the advent of European settlers who have destroyed the natives as much by introducing fire water and new diseases as by war. The effect upon happiness of such a substitution of stronger in the place of weaker races has already been partly discussed in considering the effects of the invention of the mariner's compass. For this invention led to the discovery of America, and one principal effect of that discovery has been the disappearance of the aboriginal Indians before the face of white immigrants, men of a superior race. The displacement of the Indians in America, however, had one peculiar feature in the immense increase of population which does not always accompany the extermination or diminution of weaker by stronger races. When, as in North America and Australia, the stronger conquering race is agricultural and manufacturing, while the inferior conquered race is, for the most part, composed of hunters, great increase of population is the natural result of the conquest. But this need not always be the case. The populations of Peru and Mexico may have been as great before the Spanish conquest as at the present date. So that, in some cases, even those who have made up their minds on the question in dispute between optimists and pessimists are not thereby enabled to settle whether general happiness is affected favourably or unfavourably by war between nation and nation, between race and race. Indeed, it cannot be satisfactorily determined whether war does or does not, on the whole, increase the population of the world. On the one hand, the conquering nation is probably superior

in knowledge and thereby enabled to get more production
out of the earth than the conquered. On the other hand,
the conquering nation is not unlikely to have a higher
standard of comfort which will prevent the population
from increasing in proportion to its increasing means of
subsistence. Also the prevalence of war, by withdrawing
a large proportion of the population from productive
work, tends to diminish population, and the insecurity
due to the fear of war together with the actual destruction of life and property in war has the same effect.

We must therefore, in many cases, treat the question
as if the result of war would not affect the amount of
population, and ask simply whether the average member
of a conquering race is likely to be happier than the
average member of the conquered race. Let us consider
concrete instances. Were the Jews happier than the
Canaanites? the Persians than the Assyrians? the
Greeks and Macedonians than the Persians? the Romans
than the Greeks and Carthaginians? the Saracens than
the Christians of the Eastern Empire? the Saxons than
the Britons? the Normans than the Saxons? or, looking at
the recent colonization of once savage countries by
Anglo-Saxon and other settlers, we may ask whether
they are happier than the savages whom they displace.
In the case of the last instance we can most easily
observe for ourselves, if we care to travel, the two sides
of the comparison, and without travelling we can refer
to the abundant testimony of many modern travellers.
Yet room remains for much difference of opinion.
"What a vast mass of cannibalism," remarks Sir James
Mackintosh, "was the whole population of Brazil! To
have replaced it by the most corrupt Europeans was
one of the greatest benefits to the world." But
Sir James Mackintosh had never visited savages at
home. Mr. Hume Nisbet, who in New Guinea made
the acquaintance of some of the most savage inhabitants of the world, formed a different opinion. "On

the whole," he writes in his *Land of the Hibiscus Blossom,*
" I think we civilised savages murder as much and as
atrociously as the so-called savages do in dark lands,
even though we may not eat our victims ; and, aside
from this evil, I fancy that they are happier in their
simplicity than we are with our vaunted civilisation.
. . . Looking on the savages of New Guinea from a
material standpoint, I think that they are much more comfortable as they now are than are our English poor—
indeed, than many of our English middle classes—who
are fighting so madly for an existence, while they, the
natives, bask away luxuriously on their coral-fringed
and sunny sands." It is difficult to be confident in an
opinion opposed to that of many travellers who have
passed a good part of their life among savages. But as
other travellers hold the other opinion which is more
agreeable to our feelings as civilised men, one is inclined,
though not without doubt, to believe that civilised men
are happier than savages. Perhaps we may also venture
to regard it as probable that, as a rule, conquering nations
are happier than the conquered were before the conquest,
and that, therefore, the world is happier now than it would
have been if wars had not raged in the past.

Should the utilitarian then form societies for the
encouragement of war ? He cannot reasonably do so,
unless he has reason to suppose that the increase of
happiness due to the imposition of a more orderly or
otherwise happier life on the conquered, or to the substitution of stronger in the place of weaker nations, out-
balances the accumulation of evils included in the horrors
of war. But this conviction is scarcely possible to anyone
who reads reflectively the accounts of campaigns given by
historians, and more especially by war correspondents who
have seen the dying and the dead lying before their
eyes on the bare ground, and the wretched inhabitants
of the theatre of war driven destitute out of their
burning houses. But even if the utilitarian were con-

vinced that war does on the whole more good than
harm, he would still shrink from encouraging it, and
rather exert himself to diminish its frequency.   For
war, if a good at all, is one of that class of good things
which are only good in moderation.   An individual's
health may be improved by a daily walk of five
miles, but a daily walk of thirty miles would lead
not to increased health, but to ill health.   In like
manner, though a limited amount of war might con-
ceivably be beneficial, a larger amount of war than
there has hitherto been in the world would almost
certainly be very destructive of happiness.   Therefore
the utilitarian, although of course he may approve of
particular wars waged against tyranny, will never
approve of war for its own sake, that is, for its general
consequences only.   Even if he thinks that the general
consequences of war may be good and more than out-
balance the pain it causes, he will not promote war
in the abstract, but rather discourage it, knowing
that up to the present time the angry passions of
individuals and nations have provided more than the
amount of war required gradually to eliminate inferior
races, and remembering that the useful struggle for
existence may be as effectually carried on by industrial
competition and other methods less painful than war.
Much more will he do his best to extinguish war
if he thinks, as most utilitarians probably do think, that
war in any form or amount is such a painful remedy,
that it can never, except in exceptional circumstances,
be productive of more happiness than misery.   Therefore it will be the duty of utilitarians carefully to
consider by what means war may be totally extinguished or rendered less common.

The introduction of arbitration has perhaps done
something to diminish the frequency of war, and the
utilitarian should encourage the more extensive employment of this method of settling disputes.   At the sam

time there is a danger which interferes with the pacificatory effect of all such milder substitutes for war, as long as the possibility of war remains. When war is the only means of settling national differences, nations are very careful of pressing such differences to extremity, knowing that the result may be war. But, when there is a chance of arbitration settling differences, nations may be inclined to enter into national disputes with as light a heart, as that with which some individuals enter into litigation, and yet after all eventually such angry passions may be roused that arbitration will be found impossible, and the contending parties may have to resort to war after all. However in spite of this danger arbitration may be readily supported by the utilitarian as on the whole furthering the cause of peace.

Another fact, that has diminished the amount of fighting in the world, is the tendency that has manifested itself since the beginning of history towards the division of the human race into larger and larger political aggregates. In ancient Greece, divided as it was into small states, war was terribly frequent. For each small state was surrounded by other small states, with whom it had every now and then to engage in war. Nor did these frequent small wars prevent wars on a large scale. For besides the very petty wars of one Greek state against another, there were wars like the Peloponnesian war of one confederacy of small states against another confederacy, and also national wars against Persians, Macedonians, Carthaginians, and Romans. If war were the best process of natural selection, the Greeks ought to have gone on rapidly from strength to strength, but history shows that they rapidly deteriorated in the midst of continual warfare, and probably, it may be added, because of their continual warfare. If England, France, Germany, and the other countries of Europe, were split up into small states like ancient Greece, war would be incessantly going on in modern Europe also.

E

But even as things are, in spite of arbitration and the large nations into which the world is now divided, the utilitarian will think there is too much of war, and will consider whether there are not any other means by which its comparative frequency may be diminished. One very practicable scheme for effecting this object has either been entirely overlooked or not sufficiently recognised. It is suggested by the existence of the British volunteer force. *Si vis pacem para bellum* is an old adage, and the most efficient peace-making way of preparing for war is that adopted by the British volunteers and others who strictly follow the motto, " defence not defiance." Owing to the existence of her volunteer force enlisted for the defence of her native soil in case of invasion and not for service abroad, Britain is much stronger for defensive than for offensive war. For offensive warfare, we have only our small standing army with its small reserve, while, if England were invaded, there are more than half a million of men in arms to drive out the invader. From this state of affairs, England naturally abstains from attempting to pursue an aggressive policy except sometimes in colonial wars against savage peoples, and on the other hand even the strongest foreign power is not much tempted to attack England and land an army on her coasts. The chief defect in the English volunteer force is that it is not quite large enough at present to make successful invasion impossible. If it could be increased to about one million of men, England could laugh to scorn the idea of invasion. There is no reason why this increase should not be made. Military training would, in the case of the large number of Englishmen engaged in sedentary employments, be a distinct gain. It would promote their health and happiness, and convenient times for drill and parade could be chosen, which would not interfere with peaceful avocations any more than other kinds of healthy bodily exercise. Therefore, every English utilitarian should do his best to increase the power of the volunteer force by joining it himself and inducing others to do so, and every utilitarian throughout the world should exert himself in favour of the formation of a volunteer force on the same principle in his own nation. If large enough defensive armies cannot be obtained by voluntary enlistment, let us have conscription for purely defensive purposes. When all the great powers of Europe have each one million of men enlisted for defence against invasion, and never required under any circumstances to cross the borders, a great step will have been taken to establish universal peace. For what nation would venture rashly to attack another nation with the knowledge that one million of its best soldiers could not join in the invasion, and that the invading army would be opposed by an overwhelming superiority of defensive force ?

There is another kind of struggle for existence carried on between people and people on a vast scale not by war but by industrial competition, the effect of which might be very prejudicial to happiness. This has been recognised by some nations who have, by calling in the aid of laws, tried to defend themselves against the evil effects of being worsted in such a struggle. The laws on this subject have not indeed been prompted by purely utilitarian considerations. When the United States or our Australian colonies pass laws to keep out Chinese cheap labour from their territories, they are actuated by the consideration of their own happiness alone, to which they would, if necessary, sacrifice any amount of Chinese happiness. Yet such legislation might perhaps be justified by pure utilitarian considerations. There is a real danger of the Chinese overrunning the world and everywhere underselling all industrial competitors by the smallness of the wages on which they can keep themselves in life and health. What would be the result upon general happiness if all over the world cheap yellow

labour were to take the place of our white labourers in
the field and in the workshop? The immediate result
would undoubtedly be much misery among the displaced
white workmen, who would suffer terribly from starvation and almost more from their indignation at being
driven out of existence by an inferior race of men. This
indignation would express itself in continual riots that
would inflict pain upon white assailants and still more
on the weaker yellow men. Nor would the latter feel
in their triumph happiness equivalent in amount to a
tithe of the misery suffered by the starving and indignant white men. Thus the immediate results would be
an immense amount of unmitigated misery. Nor does it
appear that there would be any ultimate good results to
compensate for all this woe. Would the happiness of the
world be found to have been permanently increased, when
the heartburnings of the displaced white worker had
been mitigated by custom or diminished in aggregate
amount by the dying out of the majority of the white
population? There is rather reason to anticipate the
contrary. In the moral elements of happiness, which
will probably be found to be more important than any
other, the Chinese seem to be decidedly inferior to
Americans, Englishmen, and continental Europeans.
Perhaps, however, this opinion may be a wrong opinion
mainly due to experience of the inferior and less respect-
able Chinamen who emigrate to America. Those who,
like the author of *The Middle Kingdom,* have lived long
in China have much to say in favour of the Chinese at
home. At any rate, we have no reason to suppose that
the Chinese are on the average happier than ourselves.
Thus the world would not be rendered permanently
happier if this very painful change, that we are considering, were effected, and, of course, on utilitarian grounds
a change painful in itself and not leading to any distinct
gain must be condemned. Therefore, utilitarian statesmen are justified in supporting laws for the exclusion of

Chinamen from territory now occupied by white men; and utilitarian Chinamen should, if they recognise the moral inferiority and consequent lesser, or not greater, happiness of their countrymen, be conservative on questions of emigration. At present old laws absolutely forbid emigration, and in consequence no women, and only such disreputable members of the community as can do without female society and have no respect for their own law and religion, emigrate. In the same way the natives of India have a religious horror of crossing the sea, by crossing which they incur guilt only to be atoned by severe penance.

But, perhaps, the change so much to be dreaded may be brought about without a native of India or China leaving his native land. Facility of communication is bringing the remotest corners of the earth into keen industrial competition with each other. Already this competition is beginning to tell with terrible effect on European agriculturalists. Corn raised by the labour of natives of India working for wages of 2d. or 3d. per day comes in large quantities into European markets, and can be sold at a price which even now renders it almost impossible for employers of agricultural labour in England and France to make any profit out of their lands. It is true that the English and French labourer does far more work in a day than an Indian can do. But the value of his work is not nearly so much more than an Indian's work as his wages are than an Indian's wages. So that the Indian's labour is really far cheaper than the European's. In such a state of affairs, which improved communication is likely to intensify, we seem to be drifting towards a time when it will only be possible profitably to grow corn in England and France on exceptionally fertile soil, and the English agricultural labourer will have to leave the plough and convert himself into a factory hand, unless he can consent to work

for an oriental labourer's pittance and subsist on vegetarian diet, forswearing his beef and beer.

But even by becoming a factory workman he will
scarcely permanently avoid the competition of cheap
oriental labour.   For in the East there are to be found
coal and iron and other materials of manufacturing
industry as well as fertile soil.   At present Asiatics
are not far enough advanced in knowledge to compete
on a large scale with European manufacturing industry.   But this ignorance will not last for ever
Already among the 250 millions of India technical
education is advancing and energetic preparations are
being made for its further extension.   Already in
Bombay cotton factories are increasing year by year,
and in the course of time the whole of India will
follow the lead of her western sea-port.   In China the
Chinese are determined to teach themselves or be taught
how to manufacture cannon and ironclads for their own
use.   Mr. James in his travels through Manchuria saw a
Chinese arsenal in which Chinese workmen without
European supervision could manufacture the most
improved instruments of destruction for themselves.   The
progressive party in China will probably before long
introduce an extended system of technical education into
their country also.   Thus in the future Chinese and
Indian workmen working for wretched wages will compete with Manchester and Glasgow on more than equal
terms.   The result of this will be just the same as if
Chinese and Indian immigrants settled in the West, and
undersold American and European labourers.   But it
cannot be well stopped by any restrictive legislation as
oriental immigration has been checked.   In the face of
this competition it is likely that the western labourer
will have to lower his standard of comfort, and work
for far lower wages than he claims at present: or else
the labouring population in the west must be reduced in
numbers to about a fourth of its present dimensions.   In

either case the world is threatened with diminution of happiness. The gradual starving out of existence of say one half of the labouring population of Europe, namely, of all the labouring population whose *raison d'être* is that Asia needs manufactured articles and cannot make them for herself, would be the result of Asiatics all over Asia obtaining mastery of all kinds of technical arts; and this starvation, though gradual, would, in the aggregate, cause about as much misery as all the famines that have been chronicled in the world's history. Perhaps less misery would be caused by the gradual lowering of the standard of comfort that would accompany the diminution of European wages down to the oriental average, especially as there would be simultaneously a gradual rise of oriental wages towards the European standard. For the new rate of wages would be somewhere between the present European and the present oriental rate. Thus the millions of Asiatics would derive from a gradual change of this kind increase of happiness, though not as much as the increase of misery on the other side of the world. But even if this, apparently the less painful, alternative be chosen, there will be much misery. Our vast labouring population will not learn to tolerate life in cold climates on vegetarian diet without much pain, and large fractions will die until only those are left who are able to adapt themselves to such very different circumstances. Whether the utilitarian can devise any means by which this change can be averted, or any reasoning by which it can be shown not to be productive of increase of misery, remains to be seen, but it is a question of such difficulty that it can hardly receive even a probable solution without more data of experience bearing upon the subject, than we at present possess.

CHAPTER VI.

"ALL work and no play makes Jack a dull boy." This old proverb expresses the belief that amusement is one of the most essential elements of happiness. If this is so, among the best practical utilitarians would seem to be those who do their utmost to spread a taste for the best games all over the world—Englishmen who teach Indians to play cricket, and Maoris to play football, Americans who introduce into the mother country their fascinating game of base-ball, rural rectors who encourage their parishioners to play cricket on the village green, and all who by precept or example induce their fellow men and fellow women to take any kind of healthy exercise in the open air. The effect upon happiness of such sports is both direct and indirect, direct inasmuch as those engaged in games enjoy themselves while playing, indirect because they lay up for themselves stores of health which may be a permanent source of happiness. There is a Spanish proverb to the effect that the days spent in hunting do not count in one's life. It means that, if a man is forty-two years old, and has spent two years in hunting, he is to all intents and purposes only forty years old, the invigorating effects of the exercise being supposed to exactly counteract the weakening effect of time. The words of this proverb may be extended so as to apply not merely to hunting but to all outdoor sports.

The case of hunting is distinguished from other means

of healthy exercise by the fact that the lower animals are forced to take part in it. Therefore the utilitarian in considering the effects of hunting upon happiness must include in his calculation the effect produced upon the hunted as well as that produced upon the hunter. Is the happiness of the lower animals injuriously affected by hunting? There is no reason to think that it is. Animals must die, and the quick violent death usually inflicted by the hunter and his hounds is less painful than the slow death by starvation or cold that the animal if unhunted would have to undergo, and not more painful than death inflicted by birds and beasts of prey. All that can be said in this connection against hunting is that animals wounded by rifle or arrow more often escape to die a lingering death than those wounded by animals of prey ; but this may be balanced by the fact that the bullet and the arrow often kill instantaneously animals that might otherwise die a longer and more painful death by hunger. It may be urged by some against hunting that an animal's life must be considered as a whole, that hunting shortens the life of many, and that, the longer their lives are, the more likely it is that the joys of life will compensate for the eventual pain of dying. This is probably true, as animals, at any rate wild animals, seem to derive more pleasure than pain from life. But on the other hand it must be remembered that hunting usually kills grown-up animals whose joy in life may be supposed to be on the wane, and leaves room for the growing up of numerous new-born animals who would otherwise be crowded out of existence for want of food. For there is no doubt that every year far more animals come into the world than the supply of food can support. Great numbers of these must die of starvation before enjoying the joys of exuberant young life. Every grown-up animal that is shot leaves room for the growth of a younger and therefore presumably happier being. Thus on the whole there is no reason to think that the happiness of lower animals is at all diminished by hunting.

This being so, it only remains to consider the effect of hunting on the happiness of human beings. At an early stage in the history of society hunting was pursued as a means of existence and not as a source of pleasure. The hunter had therefore to hunt not merely when he expected pleasure from his hunting, but at times when, if he had by him enough to eat, he would infinitely prefer bodily ease in his hut or cave. The life of a professional hunter does not seem to be in any way happier than that of a shepherd or an agricultural labourer. Nor is it more unhappy. All that we can say about the hunting stage of society is that it is incompatible with the earth being thickly peopled, so that the utilitarian pessimist has every reason to sigh for the return of the hunting stage of society. In connection with happiness we have rather to consider hunting as an occasional interlude than as the permanent occupation of a man's life. Of the intense pleasure derived from hunting both literature and the experience of life give abundant evidence. Again and again has the desire of this pleasure proved triumphant over the fear of death in tiger-shooting, fox-hunting, bear-hunting, and elephant-hunting. It drives rich men, who might take their ease in richly-furnished houses, surrounded by all the comforts supplied by wealth, to toil up the snowy mountains of the Himalayas and struggle through the hot, marshy, pestilential jungles of India, Africa, and South America. The enthusiastic love of hunting, though perhaps it reaches its highest pitch in the modern Briton, is certainly as old as civilisation and perhaps a good deal older. It has been felt by nations most widely different from each other in character. The sculptured walls of Nineveh and Babylon show the delight taken by Assyrian kings in hunting the lion, and from the dawn of civilisation in Homeric Greece to the present day a large portion of the literature of

the world has been devoted to celebrating the joys of
the chase.   Even the tyranny of feudal game laws, that
ordered the common man who killed a boar or a deer to
have his eyes torn out, and reduced great tracts of good
land to desolation that they might be the hunting-
ground of kings, helps to show the immense popularity
of hunting.

But this popularity seems at last to be somewhat on
the wane.   Evolutionists tell us that the love of hunting
is the survival of a taste that descended through many
generations of our ancestors, who, without intense con-
centration of energy on the task of killing animals, could
hardly have survived.   But the traces left on our minds
by many generations of hunting ancestors must now be
growing less distinct, as most of those now living are the
descendants for several generations back of men who
have never been engaged in hunting.   As this process of
obliteration continues, fewer and fewer men will be left so
constituted in mind as to be able to take great delight
in the chase.

There is also another influence working in the same
direction.   Human sympathy for the lower animals
is decidedly on the increase.   The society for the
prevention of cruelty to animals, though it does not
particularly direct its energy against hunting, does
indirectly discountenance any such amusement by never
allowing us to forget that the lower animals feel pain,
which is therefore not to be wantonly inflicted.   In old
times the hunter as a rule did not trouble his head about
the feelings of the hunted animal any more than about
the grass bruised under his horse's foot.   Now-a-days
this unconcern is by no means so easy.   The hunter of
to-day must often ask himself whether he is justified
in promoting his own health at the expense of so much
pain to animals, many of whom are weak and harmless.
When this troublesome question has again and again
been forced upon his mind by reading, by the teaching

of the society for the prevention of cruelty, or by the suggestion of some tender-hearted wife or sister, he is not unlikely to resolve with Wordsworth,

> Never to blend his pleasure or his pride
> With sorrow of the meanest thing that feels.

Some hunters who do not go so far as to make this resolve, cannot entirely quench the questionings of their heart, and, though they perhaps go on amusing themselves at the expense of animal pain, do so with occasional feelings of remorse which must seriously detract from the total of their pleasures. Even Scott, devoted sportsman as he was, sometimes asked himself how it came to be that

> The failing wing, the blood-shot eye
> The sportsman marks with apathy,

and the reflection must surely have marred his pleasure in the chase.

Thus Lady Florence Dixie, after shooting one of the golden deer of the Cordilleras, was so troubled in mind that she wrote, "If regret could atone for that death of which I unfortunately was the cause, then it has long ago been forgiven ; for, for many a day I was haunted by a sad remorse for the loss of that innocent and trusting life." A similar struggle of contending feelings in the hunter's breast is indicated by an incident related by J. Thomson in his account of his journey through Masai Land. "I shot," he says, "a hartebeest for the pot, and was made to regret my deed of blood on seeing the infinitely pitiful manner in which its mate hung about, divided between terror of the destroyer and wistful tenderness and anxiety for its struggling and bleeding companion. Bounding away a few steps, it would turn again to face the hunter with its great beautiful eyes, or to cast perplexed glances at the dying hartebeest, wondering, doubtless, what horrid fate had fallen upon it. I could easily have shot the poor creature, but I felt too conscience-stricken to do the deed of blood, and I let it alone." Such instances show that universal indulgence in hunting cannot be advocated as productive of happiness in spite of its general good effects upon health, For the happiness due to improved health may be cancelled by the pains of an uneasy conscience.

Should the utilitarian even encourage in this amusement those who, from bluntness of feeling or want of reflection, are able to derive unalloyed enjoyment from the chase? Even this is doubtful. Many will be of opinion that it is essential in the interests of happiness that universal sympathy with all living beings should be aimed at, and that the promotion of this universal sympathy is of far more importance to happiness than the coarse pleasure that unreflective persons derive from pursuing and killing animals, and from the more refined pleasures that attend the chase. Such persons should be taught sympathy, by being continually reminded that the lower animals feel pain or pleasure just as we do, though probably to a less intense degree. It may, however, be urged in favour of hunting, that after all, as pointed out above, hunting does not diminish animal happiness, and that, therefore, a reasonable person who clearly recognises this truth may go on hunting without feeling that he is gaining pleasure at the expense of animal pain. Perhaps a perfectly logical being might do so, but as men are constituted with their emotions continually usurping a position in the realm of reason, it seems impossible for men to inflict death and cruel wounds on sentient beings without doing violence to their sympathetic feelings.

Thus the settlement of this question must be deferred until the effects upon happiness of extended sympathy have to be considered. In the meantime we must consider those many other out-door amusements which, like hunting and shooting, are often very enjoyable in themselves and promote the health of their votaries, but do not inflict pain on animals. The chief of such amusements are cricket, football, lawn-tennis, racquets, fives, riding, swimming, baseball, skating, bicycling, tricycling.

In this great variety we find out-door active amusements to suit every purse, and almost every taste. Even the poorest man, if he lives in the country, can generally find some beautiful river or seashore open to him as a bathing place, and, at the worst, he can always walk, enjoying the companionship of some dear friend, or silently admiring the beauties of the country, or in great cities the wonderful works of man. Walking only requires a little extra expense in soleing and heeling boots, and some other outdoor amusements, such as skating and football, are almost equally inexpensive. There can be no doubt that on the whole they immensely improve the health of those who are addicted to them. Occasionally a man may be maimed for life by an accident in the cricket field or at football. A few Oxford or Cambridge oars may overstrain themselves by violent exercise in the boat race, or the severe preliminary training they have to undergo. But the number of such casualties is immensely exaggerated by the publicity given to them in the press. When reckless assertions about the evil effects of rowing upon rowing men were being made in the papers, Dr. J. E. Morgan, who had a truly Baconian distrust of affirmative instances, took the trouble to look up the life-history of those who had rowed in the world-famous University boat-race. The result of his enquiries was the discovery that their average of life and health was decidedly better than that of ordinary men. If the pain caused by accidents in active out-door amusements were compared with the increase of happiness they confer on the thousands who do not happen to meet with any accident, they would be found to be as nothing in the balance. The contrary opinion could never have been held, but for the tendency to see clearly pain that is concentrated in a few individuals, and to ignore the mass of happiness far greater in the aggregate that is scattered over a large multitude though not conspicuously evident in any of the individual members of the multitude. When the imperceptible growth of thousands of trunks, myriads of branches, and millions of twigs, is taken into consideration, we recognise that the amount of timber in a forest has increased in the course of a year, though a few branches, or even whole trees, may have been blown down by the wind. In the same way we should recognise that the thousands of men and women who pursue enjoyment in active open-air games have vastly increased their happiness, even though a small minority may have hurt themselves by unfortunate accidents, or imprudent excess in their out-door activity.

But those who add to their health and happiness by energetically engaging in out-door recreation are only a fraction, and perhaps a small fraction of the whole world. We must now consider whether it necessarily follows that the general happiness has been advanced because the happiness of this fraction has been advanced. We have seen reason to believe that though medical science improves the health and happiness of individuals, it does not generally improve the health and happiness of the whole race. Can the same disparagement be justly applied to the source of happiness that we are now considering? Or is there any essential difference between out-door exercise and medical curative drugs, operations, diet, &c., on account of which we can say that, while the latter benefit individuals without benefiting the human race, the former benefits the race as much as the individual? There does seem to be such a difference. It consists in the fact that out-door athletic games are eagerly engaged in by the healthy and avoided by the delicate,

while medical drugs, diet, and surgical operations are
more usually prescribed for and used by the delicate than
by the healthy. We saw that the chief evil of medical
science from the point of view of general happiness was
that it enabled human beings who would otherwise have
died childless to survive and transmit their delicacy to
their descendants. This bad effect does not arise from
out-door exercise at any rate in its more violent forms.
A moderate walk of two or three miles a day may benefit the individual delicate man as much as or more than
carefully regulated diet or well-chosen drugs. But if
the very delicate man attempts football, hunting, Alpine
climbing, or big game shooting, it is likely very much
to diminish the few years he would otherwise live, and
is more likely to reduce the moderately delicate man
to the level of the very delicate than to raise the very
delicate man to the level of the moderately delicate.
Thus these violent delights tend to strengthen the
strong, while they debilitate the weak and drive them
rapidly out of existence. Out-door amusements have
also another advantage over medical appliances, particularly over medical drugs. Surgical operations are
painful, and most medical drugs are nauseous. But
out-door exercise is not only productive of health, but
also delightful in itself. Thus it is doubly conducive
to pleasure, and those who exert themselves successfully
in establishing football clubs, Alpine clubs, cricket, and
rowing clubs, and by other means promote a taste for
the more violent athletic out-door amusements, do really
substantially promote the utilitarian end.

Another class of amusements deserves careful consideration on the part of the utilitarian, namely, those
kinds of recreation which are not accompanied by
active bodily exertion. The chief pleasures of this kind
are those afforded by the fine arts, especially painting,
sculpture, and music. Looked at from a utilitarian
point of view, they differ from the pleasures of active

bodily exercise in two respects. They do not tend to kill off the weak, and they have little effect, as compared with out-door sports, in strengthening the strong. They can be enjoyed as much by the delicate as by the healthy, and improve the health of the delicate. The first difference tends to make the kind of pleasures we are now considering less productive of the general happiness than the pleasures of active bodily exercise. Nevertheless, while it is clear that they do not do nearly so much to improve the health of the strong, it would be a mistake to suppose that they do nothing. Whatever relieves the mind of the worker from the burden of earning money, or the vacant idler from the monotony of a purposeless existence, promotes cheerfulness and thereby promotes health. But still the active out-door sports have the advantage, as they not only promote cheerfulness, but also improve the health in a far more effectual way by bracing the muscles and keeping us in the open air.

For one class, however, the pleasures of the fine arts are preferable as a means of relaxation. It is possible even for a healthy man to have too much hard work in the open air. The agricultural labourer, the postman, the railway porter, the groom and others, who are fortunate enough to earn their livelihood by open air work, cannot be expected to devote much of their leisure time to football, or cricket. Their muscles and lungs being sufficiently provided for by their working life, they should be taught to turn to the fine arts for recreation. To supply their needs, the utilitarian should provide museums, picture galleries, concert rooms, zoological and botanical gardens, and they should be open on Sundays and week-day evenings, in order that they may be used not merely by those keeping holyday, but also by busy men in their short intervals of leisure. In the country sufficient beauty is provided for the eye by nature. But in the man-made town too often

F

the beauty of nature has disappeared without any architectural beauty being brought in to compensate for the loss. In great cities the utilitarian has plenty of good work to do. Parks have to be made and defended against the attacks of so-called utilitarians, who would like to see them covered over with houses and factories. It is one of the evils of private property that too much beautiful scenery is kept for the enjoyment of the few and denied to the many. Many rich men entirely refuse the public access to their grounds.

> " Why should not these great Sirs
> Give up their parks some dozen times a year
> To let the people breathe ?"

If utilitarians have extensive grounds near a great city, they should throw them open to the public, or, at least, if they are not extensive enough to become promenades, allow the weary walker along the dusty roads to refresh his eyes by looking into them through railings. At present in the suburbs of great towns it is too often the practice to protect gardens and pleasure grounds against intrusive eyes by high walls or hideous barriers of tarred or untarred planks. This abominable selfishness compels the unfortunate citizen to walk miles out into the country, before he can see anything pleasanter to look on than the dusty or muddy road, and should surely be strongly condemned by public opinion.

Material should also be provided for the ear by the utilitarian. Concerts can be organised at low rates, and public rooms may be presented with pianos or harmoniums. Much good work in this direction has been done by the Gordon League, " a body of benevolent individuals who shortly after General Gordon's death formed themselves into a league, to carry on under the auspices of his great name the work of mercy in which he delighted." Besides attending to the material wants of the poor by forming coal funds and clothing funds, they provide excellent gratuitous concerts at their head quarters in the Portman Rooms. "Every Sunday evening," we read in a daily paper, "at half past eight o'clock when the churches are closed, the doors of the Portman Rooms are thrown open to working men and women for a social gathering. There is no Sabbath glumness at these meetings, the League recognising that no hard-and-fast line should be drawn between sacred things and those which are called secular, but that everything good and pure is consecrated by use for worthy ends. Hence the Sunday evening meetings happily associate the religion of Christianity with that of common life. Members of the League sing appropriate songs to their congregation, or play instrumental solos, or give recitations inciting to high and noble deeds, or read the Bible, and lead the psalm or hymn. In this manner the poor are attracted within the influence of much that makes for their peace. As a rule about 1,000 people attend each Sunday evening, most of them being precisely those on whose behalf the Gordon net is spread. Last evening the seats in the spacious hall were well filled by a most orderly and attentive crowd, whose behaviour, we are bound to say, might advantageously be taken as a model by not a few calling themselves their betters. The efforts honestly made to please them were keenly appreciated and loudly applauded." Similar attempts are made in the same spirit in different parts of the country to provide instrumental and vocal music for the poor. They are valuable not merely for the immediate pleasure they confer on the audiences, and as counter attractions rivalling the less innocent pleasures of the public house or gambling den, but also as establishing kindliness between rich and poor, and softening the asperity of the envy with which the latter often regard the former. Also at such meetings a taste for music may be acquired which may be cultivated in many an otherwise dull home as a perennial source of innocent pleasure.

There is, however, a drawback in all attempts to provide the poor with entertainments of a charitable character. This cannot be better expressed than in the words of Mr. G. R. Sims, a writer who has done much to reveal the misery of the London poor, and interpret their feelings. " The well-meaning efforts," he tells us, " of the societies which have endeavoured to attract the poor to hear countesses fiddle and baronets sing comic songs in temperance halls, have not been crowned with anything like success, for the simple reason that there is an air of charity and goody goody about the scheme, which the poor always regard with suspicion. They want their amusement as a right, not as a favour, and they decline to be patronized."

This objection, fortunately, does not apply to another species of musical entertainment within the reach of everybody. It is probable that the poor derive the greatest amount of pleasure, through the ear, from a humble and much-despised source, namely, from the ubiquitous organ-grinder, who spreads all over London familiarity with tunes new and old. Many an air is thus picked up by errand boys and workmen on their way to their work, and they solace their hours of labour by humming and whistling snatches of song, which, but for the street-organ, they would never have known. Let us then un-grudgingly pay our pennies to encourage those wandering minstrels by whose instrumentality the airs, which sung by Patti or Albani delight the rich man in his opera-box, give even more delight to the poor street arab.

Music, even good music, seems to give pleasure without any previous training. It is different with some of the other fine arts. Sculpture, for instance, may almost be regarded as an acquired taste. The average British workman does not derive very much pleasure from the sculptures of the British Museum, and even the more educated crowds, who visit the Royal Academy, do not much frequent the sculpture gallery. In the case of sculpture, and to a less extent in the case of painting, it is necessary to cultivate taste among the masses, and this is not easily done. Some effect is undoubtedly produced by simply placing paintings and sculptures before their eyes, but this needs to be supplemented by a certain amount of instruction in art. No doubt Ruskin's *Modern Painters* has taught many to appreciate art who would otherwise have remained artistically blind. Such literary works then promote the happiness of the world, if the fine arts themselves promote happiness.

But before we arrive at an ultimate conclusion on the latter question we have to give full weight to the effect of the cultivation of the fine arts on the population of the world. The workers who produce beautiful objects for the gratification of the senses, in so far as they merely produce beauty, are unproductive consumers, and, therefore, their presence in the world diminishes the population of the world. If all painters, musicians, sculptors, engravers, poets, manufacturers of ribbons and ornamental cloth, jewellers, makers of fine porcelain, carvers in wood and ivory, and others who produce beautiful objects or beautify useful objects, and in addition all those who manufacture instruments or obtain materials for beautiful work-manship as the makers of musical instruments, of painters' colours, of sculptors', engravers', wood-carvers', and jewellers' tools, and elephant hunters, and miners in ruby and diamond mines, were all to turn their energies to reclaiming waste land or any other distinctly productive work, the world would be able to support a far larger population than it does now. This being the case, pessimist utilitarians should strive hard to promote the fine arts, as the pursuit of them diminishes the number of miserable beings in the world and at the same time makes the average man less miserable. Optimist utilitarians cannot so easily decide the question. They must allow that the fine arts diminish the number of happy beings in the world, but must go on to consider whether the increase in average happiness does or does not more than compensate for that loss. Thus, if without the fine arts the population of the world would be 1,500,000,000 and the average happiness 100°, and with the fine arts the average happiness is 105° and the population is 1,400,000,000, he would prefer that the fine arts should be entirely stamped out, as with the fine arts the aggregate happiness would be only 147,000,000,000°, while without it the sum would be 150,000,000,000°. The utilitarian who leans neither to pessimism nor optimism would prefer to promote the fine arts, because not having made up his mind whether the average man is happy or miserable, he is indifferent whether the number of human beings is greater or smaller, and is bound to favour whatever promotes the average happiness.

CHAPTER VII.

In considering the effect of law and custom upon happiness, we have to consider first whether good laws and good constitutions increase the happiness of the world. Have such lawgivers as Lycurgus, Solon, Justinian, and the authors of the code Napoleon or legislative bodies like the English House of Commons had great opportunities of increasing happiness and how far have they used those opportunities well? If a good code of laws increases the happiness of particular nations, it may be assumed to increase the happiness of the world. For, if happiness is by means of good laws secured for one nation, there is no reason to believe that the gain is secured at the expense of any other nation. Although in the assignment of punishment some suppose that just retribution is a paramount consideration, the promotion of happiness is generally regarded as the great end of the art of jurisprudence : so that jurisprudence may almost be regarded as a branch of utilitarian ethics. This being the case, it is not surprising to find eminent lawyers like Bentham and Austin among the staunchest upholders of utilitarian morality, for, when they pass from jurisprudence to morality, they only change from a more limited to a more general survey of the means of promoting happiness. Although it is generally recognised that the goodness of laws and constitutions is relative, that what suits one nation may be unsuitable to another, there is little or no doubt in the opinion of the world that national happiness may be promoted by good laws and constitutions. Plato is so convinced of the fact that he makes it the foundation on which to build his proof of the happiness of the good man. One of the premises of his reasoning in the main argument of the Republic is that the most perfectly constituted state is sure to be more productive of happiness than a worse constituted state. Others, however, are of the opinion of Pope's couplet :—

> For forms of government let fools contest,
> Whate'er is best administered is best.

To exhaustively consider this question would be to write a book on jurisprudence. It is, however, possible to come to a conclusion on the subject by a shorter route. That legal and constitutional reform does beneficially affect happiness will be seen clearly enough. Even if a nation may be happy in spite of bad laws and a bad constitution, it would surely be still happier with good laws and a good constitution. Pope's antithetical couplet may be easily shown not to prove his point, even if we admit the statement made in the second line. Granting that the government that is best administered is best, it is surely plain that some forms of government are more likely to be well administered than others. This truth was recognised by Solon when he defended himself against a critic by observing that his laws were not ideally the best, but only the best that he thought he could get the Athenians to obey. One or two conspicuous instances in history are enough to make it clear to any unprejudiced mind that legislative changes may much promote the happiness of a people, especially perhaps repeals of bad laws or changes in the constitution of courts of justice. He would be a bold man who would deny that the Great Charter, the Habeas Corpus Act, and the repeal of laws opposed to the principle of religious toleration have done much for the happiness of England. Like good effects were produced by the laws of Solon in Greece, and in Rome by the laws which amicably settled the bitter contentions between the Patricians and Plebeians.

The discussion of the effect that can be produced on happiness by particular political measures has to a large extent been anticipated in the previous pages. The laws may establish national schools, national colleges, and national museums, where the poor can be educated gratis. This will undoubtedly increase knowledge, and, if increase of knowledge implies increase of happiness, happiness will be increased by such laws, or would be but for one difference between spread of knowledge by private effort and by legal enactment. Laws establishing a cheap gratuitous system of public education are in accordance with the socialistic or semisocialistic principle that the rich should be taxed for the benefit of the poor. Whether the carrying out of this principle is productive of happiness or not, is a question on which much difference of opinion prevails. Possessors of wealth will generally urge that the taxation of the rich for the poor discourages accumulation of capital, diminishes the wage fund, increases want, and diminishes industry and happiness. The poor, and the friends of the poor on the other hand, only recognise the fact that gratuitous education satisfies the yearnings of many who would otherwise grow up ignorant, and, owing to their ignorance, be liable to be ground down by poverty. Similar arguments are brought forward on either side in discussing the imposition of a graduated income-tax and laws limiting the freedom of bequests or heavily taxing large legacies, the socialistic tendency of which is more clearly discernible. Laws of this character undoubtedly discourage the accumulation of capital, or drive it to other countries where such laws are not made. With the latter result, though it may be deplorable from a patriotic point of view, the utilitarian has nothing to do, unless he has good reason to believe

that it is better for the happiness of the world that
capital should be accumulated in his own rather than in
some foreign country. Of course, he must not make up
his mind upon this point without carefully purging his
intellect from patriotic bias. If he comes to the un-
patriotic conclusion that capital promotes happiness
more in other countries than his own, he will, of course,
be inclined to support any laws that drive capital into
foreign countries. As to the diminution or less increase
of capital brought about by such laws in the country in
which they are passed, there can be little doubt that it
is a fact. An ordinary mortal will be less inclined to
save than to spend, if the more he saves the greater is
the proportion of his property that he will be forced to
pay to government in the form of taxes, and if he is
much limited in exercising what he is inclined to regard
as the sacred right of doing what he likes with his own.
In the case of free education, the diminution of capital
due to discouragement of saving, may be compensated
for, or more than compensated for, by the increased
productiveness secured by the spread of education among
the masses. Knowledge being power, increased education enables man to get more out of nature. Also,
education not only produces good sense that will lead to
greater thrift, but also, as we have seen, diminishes the
number of wasteful riots and rebellions. These considerations render it probable, that, after all, although free
education means that the rich must educate not only his
own children, but also those of the poor, and so discourages saving, it may nevertheless, on the whole,
produce increase of capital.

But is the accumulation of capital productive of
happiness ? Political economy will not allow us now to
believe with Dr. Johnson that the extravagant waste of
the rich is a benefit to the poor. We all know now, that
the miser who saves and invests his money provides more
wages for poor labourers than the extravagant spend-

thrift. So, if accumulation of capital is a good thing for happiness, laws of a socialistic tendency should be avoided, and we should rather, if strict justice is an unattainable ideal, have income taxes graduated so as to tax the poor more than the rich. But, although it is clear that the accumulation of capital increases population, it is not clear that such accumulation promotes happiness. We are at this point brought back to the old question between optimists and pessimists. Pessimists should regard the increase of population, the increase of miserable beings in the world, as an evil almost sure to result eventually from accumulation of capital, although recognising that it may effect a temporary good by increasing the amount of subsistence, temporary because the population is likely to increase in a very short time till it reaches the greater number that the increased subsistence allows to live. They will also be inclined to think that the numerous masses suffer a great deal of pain from a warranted or unwarranted sense of injustice at seeing the peculiar advantages enjoyed exclusively by the few rich, and that this pain of the many is far greater in the aggregate than the pain from a sense of injustice that would be suffered by the much smaller number of rich at seeing themselves the objects of special legislation, and being compelled to pay out of their property a larger fraction as taxes than the poor are required to pay. Owing to these considerations the pessimist utilitarian ought to be in favour of socialistic legislation. The optimist, on the contrary, seeing that socialism, by depriving those who are industrious and inclined to save of their reward, would decrease the population of the world, ought to be strongly opposed to socialism. At any rate, we may rest assured that the optimist has stronger reasons to oppose socialism than can be brought forward by the pessimist.

The same may be said with even greater confidence in the case of free trade. The corn-laws were repealed in 1846. From 1855 to 1885 the population of the United Kingdom rose from 27,800,000 to 36,300,000. There is no doubt that free trade largely contributed to this great increase of population, and that, if it were more generally adopted, the world would produce more, and so be able to support a still larger population. Political economists show quite clearly that, when trade is free, each country works at the production of whatever it can best produce, while protection is a waste of labour, as it makes a nation produce what might be best produced by some other nation. Free trade may diminish the happiness of the nation that adopts it, if that nation's circumstances cause some very unpleasant industry to be the work which it can most productively engage in. Thus some, who, like Ruskin, think, and are perhaps right in thinking, that agricultural life is happier than labour in factories, may suppose that England loses happiness by free trade, as thereby a very large proportion of her children are condemned to work in mines and ironworks. If this is the case, England's loss is some other nation's gain, for England's devotion to mining and manufactures enables some other nation to addict itself more to agriculture, and thus the happiness of the world is not affected. So that if free trade affect to any great extent the happiness of the world, it does so by increasing the world's inhabitants, and so adding to the aggregate happiness, if the average man is happy, or to the aggregate misery, if the average man is unhappy.

Another way in which free trade may perhaps affect happiness, though only in a slight degree, is by producing monotony of occupation in particular regions. The more the principle of free trade is followed, the more the world will be mapped out into corn-producing regions, mining regions, regions in which iron is manufactured, and so on. Certainly such monotony of occupation is unpleasant in itself, and must also produce narrow-mindedness, and cramp the human intellect, and may so diminish happiness ; if it can be proved that happiness is at all in proportion to knowledge. But this is rather a minor consideration. A seemingly more serious way in which free trade, by tending to limit particular areas of the world to particular industries, may be prejudicial to happiness is that it may intensify the horrors of war. A country dependent on foreign countries for many of the necessaries of life may suffer terrible privation when debarred by an enemy from external commerce. Of this danger the United Kingdom is a conspicuous example, since owing to free trade we import yearly 146,000,000 bushels of wheat and only produce about half that amount. The corn produced in England annually is not nearly enough to feed the teeming population. It follows from this state of affairs that, if Britain should ever be blockaded by a superior naval enemy, the sufferings of the population from starvation would be terrible. The same is true in a less degree of many other countries partially dependent on foreign supplies. Thus free trade tends to intensify the horrors of war. But perhaps this is after all not an evil. The more horrible war is, the more nations will keep the peace, and the more quickly wars will be finished. So that free trade while intensifying the horrors of war would seem to tend to make wars less frequent and of less duration.

As this effect and that of the cramping of ideas have no very great influence on happiness, the consideration of free trade for the most part drives us back to the old open question between optimism and pessimism. For the same reason that should make optimists discourage and pessimists encourage socialistic reforms, optimists should approve and pessimists disapprove of such a powerful means of increasing population as free trade is.

Limitation by law of the amount of labour stands on much the same footing as protection, inasmuch as by limiting production it tends to keep down the population of the world. It is looked upon by many friends of the poor as a panacea for the woes of the working classes. They suppose that it will improve the lot of the labourer, firstly, by lightening the burden of men's work, by protecting women against unsuitable work, and by saving young children from having to work at other than their school tasks, and secondly by diminishing production and so enabling labour to be more profitable and to secure higher prices. These were the objects aimed at by the Swiss Government when they invited the European Governments to meet at Berne in September, 1889, to consider the labour question. Their programme included, first, prohibition of Sunday labour; secondly, fixation of a minimum age for the admission of children to factories; thirdly, fixation of a maximum for the daily labour of young workmen; fourthly, prohibition of the employment of women and young workmen in such industries as are specially injurious to health; fifthly, limitation of night labour for women and young workmen; and sixthly, stipulations for the execution of the Convention to be eventually concluded. Usually such schemes include a definite proposal to limit the hours of work to eight hours daily. All the proposals tend to have, and are intended to have the same result, namely, lessening of the burden of daily work and diminution of production.

The following considerations will make it clear that the increase of wages hoped for from the diminution of production is a vain hope, and that such proposals, if approved of at all, must be so solely because they lighten the over heavy average burden of labour. The only way in which diminution of production could increase the profits of labour is, if it were confined to some single industry productive of a necessary of life for which no substitute could be found, and if production in that industry were limited all over the world. For instance, if coal-miners all over the world agree to work only six hours a day in order to limit production of coal, the price of coal would rise perhaps so high that the miners would get as high wages for six hours' work as they now get for a full day's work. But even under such improbable circumstances, these high wages, which, after all, would not be high absolutely, but only in comparison with the amount of work done, could not long be maintained. Even if the high price of coal did not fall before increased production of petroleum and other substitutes, labourers would desert other industries and crowd into coal-mining in order to get good wages for short hours of work, and this competition would infallibly bring down the wages of coal mining, until the miners were paid very much less for their six hours than they used to be paid for their full day's work. Thus even under the most favourable conditions the policy of limited production would, far from better-ing the condition of the working classes, lead to their getting a smaller amount of wages daily.

It may be urged on the contrary that trades unions can sometimes prevent the competition of outside labourers, and that thus the coal miners might, in the case we are considering, receive for their half day's work almost as much as the wages before given for a full day's work. This is true, but does not affect the question from a general point of view. The gain of the coal miners in this case would be at the expense of all other wage earners, who in the matter

of the purchase of coal would have the value of
their wages diminished by the success of the coal
miners.

So far we have been considering limitation of hours
of work and consequently of production all over the
world in one particular industry. If the limitation
were confined to one country, the labourers would,
unless their industry were fostered at the expense
of other wage earners by heavy protective duties,
entirely fail of their objects, and be thrown out of
employment. For capital would be transferred to
other countries where such limitations did not prevail.
If the coal miners in England banded together to
work only six hours a day to limit the output of
coal, capital now engaged in English coal-mining
would immediately be transferred to German and
other coal mines where it would be employed more
profitably, unless the English coal miners were willing
to receive half wages for their half day's work, a
contingency so utterly opposed to the purpose aimed
at by the limitation of production that it need not
be considered. The same result would happen if the
limitation of production were extended to all the
industries of one country, say England. In that case
there would be an immense transfer of capital out of
England into other countries, whose wage fund would
be increased at the expense of England, so that the
average wages of the world would not be increased
and the general happiness would receive no benefit.
England in this case would suffer severely for want
of capital, unless the labourers consented to receive
small pay, as the Hindus do, in proportion to the small
production of each man's short daily labour. The
cogency of these considerations is recognized even by
some of the most thorough-going friends of the
working man, as by Mr. Bradlaugh, who desires wages
to be as high, and days of labour as short as is

compatible with profitable industry, but objects to
legislative action establishing a universal eight hours'
day of work, on the grounds that if " eight hours'
labour be translated to mean, that no works of any
description are to be conducted for more than eight
hours in each twenty-four hours, the giving legal
effect to a prohibition of this kind would be certainly
ruinous to many of the largest industries in this
country," and that, " to prevent men in all kinds
of labour from working more than eight hours
out of twenty-four may, and in some cases would,
involve a serious reduction of the wages hitherto
received."

On account of the necessity of such results, schemes
for the diminution of production by lessening the hours
of labour of the men and the amount of work done
by women and children, are by some of their advocates intended to extend to the whole world. Such
a universal extension of the limitation of labour in
the present state of the world is chimerical. There
would be little hope of arriving at an international
agreement to include China, Japan, India, the Republics
of South America and the whole world. But, even if
it could be arranged, no benefit would accrue to the
labouring classes, at least, not the anticipated benefit
of higher wages. If such a world-embracing scheme
were realized, the diminished supply would not be
enough for the demand, and, therefore, it is supposed
that the labours of production would be better rewarded. But those who argue thus, forget that pro-
ducers are also consumers, and that the possibility of
making large profits owing to the scarcity of their
production would be defeated by the corresponding
scarcity of what they themselves require, tools for
their work, and food and clothing, and other necessaries and luxuries. Under these circumstances, even
if the labourer got larger money wages, he would be

G

able to buy so much less for the same amount of
money that he would not be benefited. From a
consideration of this fact, Jevons goes to the very
opposite extreme, and asserts that "a real increase of
wages to the people at large, is to be obtained only
by making things cheaply," that is, by increasing the
produce of labour. But this seems to ignore the fact
that cheapness of products leads to increase of population, which increase tends to lower wages by increasing the supply of labourers. The fact seems to
be that neither diminution of production nor increase
of production can clearly be shown to improve wages
permanently. On the whole perhaps it would be
better to increase than to diminish production, as
diminution of production would cause a temporary
diminution of happiness until the population of the
world adjusted itself to the diminished production,
and this adjustment would not be effected without
much misery and starvation. When the new state
of affairs that would be introduced by universal
diminution of production is established, we shall
only have, instead of a larger population receiving
larger pay for more work, a smaller population
receiving a smaller amount of pay for less work.
So the advantage to happiness of lighter work
would be cancelled by the disadvantage of insufficient food.

Thus the optimist utilitarian at any rate should
not advocate limitation of labour. Perhaps the pessimist might be moved to do so on account of the
diminution of the world's population, making allowance, however, for temporary misery caused by the
adjustment of the population to the limited production. The majority of the world who are neither
optimists nor pessimists should join with the optimist
in maintaining the *status quo.*

The foregoing remarks mainly apply to the diminution of the daily labour of men. They also apply, but in a less degree, to limitation of the labour of women and children, as that limitation also diminishes production. At any rate, more is produced when not only men but also women work. The case of young children is different. If they work in factories, they cannot be properly educated, and their intelligence suffers, and want of intelligence diminishes production. But whether production is limited or not by regulation of the labour of women and children, the utilitarian should give such regulation his support. The sacrifice of happiness involved in mothers engaging in hard work, and leaving their infants to be fed on artificial food, and their homes to take care of themselves, and in depriving childhood of the pleasant alternation of school and play is very great, far greater than the misery suffered by over-worked men; and, after all, the labours of women and children do not to any appreciable extent lighten the labours of husband and father. Of course, a man and a woman can earn more than a man can by himself, and even young children may add a pittance to the family income. This knowledge makes the poor labourer accept lower wages or marry earlier, as he hopes that his wife will add to his earning, and that, if he has any children, they will at a very early age contribute to their own support. But such early marriages prevent the labours of women and children from raising the standard of comfort among labourers, who, if they have to depend on their own exertions, and therefore marry later, are as well off as if they married early in the hope of being partly supported by their wives and children. Early marriage, rendered possible by wife and children being allowed to over-task themselves in physical labour, does not seem to be desirable. Under such circumstances, domestic happiness must be extinguished in the necessity of heavy labour laid upon weak and strong alike. Therefore, no utilitarian is likely to blame the factory laws of England, which, for the most part leaving grown-up men to themselves, protect women and children against excessive work, and do not allow very young children to work at all. Such legislation might profitably be carried to further extremes, if the nations adopting it could be protected by some such international agreement as that proposed by Switzerland against the danger of being undersold by other nations who do not put the same restrictions upon labour.

But though limitation of production would not really better the condition of the working classes even if it gave the labourer higher money wages, is it not possible by any means to increase the real reward as opposed to the pecuniary wages of the working man? Co-operation, trades unions, and strikes are the usual means employed for the attainment of this object. Now there is no doubt that determined strikes have often produced increase in wages, and so bettered the condition of the workmen. On the other hand it is equally certain that many strikes, especially unsuccessful strikes, have dissipated the savings of poor workers and so reduced them to poverty. These two good and bad effects may be regarded from a working man's point of view as about balancing each other. But what from the same point of view should incline the balance in favour of strikes is the good effected by the fear of strikes. It is this that prevents the capitalist employer all over Europe from venturing to pay very low wages to his workmen when he is himself making very high profits, in case he should thereby be involved in a ruinous contest with them. This fear will not, however, make him pay such high wages as would deprive him of the average rate of profit on capital, and, if the men insist upon an exces-

sively high rate of wages, he will withdraw his capital
from the business, unless he can get higher prices out
of the consumer. It is hardly likely that he will be
able to sell as much goods at the higher as at the
lower price, so he will produce fewer goods, and
employ a less amount of labour, and transfer much of
his capital to other industries in England or to foreign
countries, where the rate of wages allows larger profits. In many cases capitalists would take away their
whole capital from the business they had, before the
strike, been employing it in. If this determination to
get higher wages than will, without increasing the
price of the goods sold, allow the ordinary rate of
profit, should extend over the whole of England, much
capital would be transferred to foreign countries,
where labour could be obtained for lower wages.
Thus capital would only be employed in England
in industries in which higher prices could be got
from the consumer. English work would be hopelessly
undersold in foreign markets, and to a large extent
in home markets also, unless importation of foreign
goods were prevented by high protective duties.
Thus the state of affairs would be that there would
be in England a few labourers enjoying high wages,
and an immense number of unemployed, who would
perish of destitution until the population should be
reduced to the small number that could get employment under the new state of affairs. Whether the
eventual condition of the labouring population would
be worse or better than it is now, would be hard to
determine ; but it is certain that the reduction in
their numbers could not be effected without much
misery.

The only way in which strikes could secure higher
wages, than without alteration of prices would allow
the average rate of profits, is by a harmonious determination all over the world among the working classes

to demand higher wages. In this case capitalists, having no foreign country with lower wages to transfer their capital to, might consent to take less profit. If all European labourers could come to some such agreement, how could the same sentiment of resistance to the claims of capital be instilled into the Chinese and Hindoo labourer? Would they not be likely rather to jump at the increased employment in agricultural and manufacturing industries opened up to them by the obstinacy of their European rivals? If, however, in the future, by improved communication, the working classes all over the world can combine for concerted action, they may win for themselves at the expense of the capitalist's profits much higher wages than they now have. Let us consider then whether such a result would promote the sum of human happiness.

The question may to a certain extent be answered by appeals to experience. Wages are very high in America and Australia, very low in India. Is the average happiness of mankind much greater in America and Australia than it is in India? The question would be hard to answer. The difference between the climate, religion, and political position of India and of those two countries is so great that, if any difference in happiness could be traced, it would be rash to attribute it to difference in the rate of wages. It would be more to the purpose to compare the happiness of England and the United States, because, although there is less difference between the average wages of England and the United States than between the average wages of India and the United States, England and the United States very closely resemble each other in climate, religion, government and other conditions, on which happiness mainly depends. On the whole, life would appear to be happier or less miserable in North America than it is in England. At least this is the conclusion indicated by the comparative estimates of travellers and by the doubtful evidence of suicide. From the suicide statistics collected by Morselli it appears that suicide is about twice as common in England as in the United States. This superiority in happiness of Americans over Englishmen may most naturally be ascribed to the higher wages obtained by the working classes.

Yet it has sometimes been maintained on various plausible grounds that high wages do not promote happiness. It is often said, for instance, that, when labouring men get a spell of high wages, they squander it recklessly on champagne and other ridiculous extravagances. But such lamentable waste is rather the result of the unusualness of high wages than of high wages in themselves. If workmen were more used to high wages, they would look upon them as ordinary income to be spent on useful things, rather than as a temporary windfall to be quickly squandered. Even if these occasional outbursts of extravagance are not exaggerated by critics devoid of sympathy with the working-classes and inclined to concentrate attention exclusively on their failings, they are not quite so painful in their effects as the ruinous extravagance committed by so many ill-paid labourers, who now spend the most of their pittance on gin, when they themselves and their wives and children are starving for want of bread. Others, who cannot be accused of want of sympathy with the working-classes, are disposed to depreciate the good effect of such material advantages as high wages. Mr. Booth, in his valuable work on " East London," says that " An analysis of the elements of happiness would hardly be in place here, but it may be remarked that neither poverty nor wealth have much part in it. The main conditions of human happiness I believe to be work and affection, and he who works for those he loves

fulfils these conditions most easily." But the men
whose work earns for those they love the barest
possible subsistence, and who are threatened with
starvation or the work-house at the least reverse,
and who have little prospect of laying by anything
for their old age, are surely under such circumstances only rendered more miserable or less happy
by having loved ones dependent on their labours.
No doubt, even in such circumstances, custom, the
great equaliser of the happiness and misery of men,
can alleviate their sufferings, but this alleviation cannot
amount to extinction of pain, especially when they
compare their lot with those who seem to do no work,
or far less work, and yet have no fear for the future.
But do not those earning a miserable pittance derive
satisfaction from comparing their lot with the still
more miserable condition of the unemployed ?   No.
For the misery of the unemployed is the very prospect that enhances their misery, as the least misfortune is liable to hurl them into the same abyss,
while they have very little hope of rising to a
higher stratum of society by any stroke of good
fortune.

Some one may object that in considering the effect
of high wages on general happiness we must consider
how it affects, not merely the working-classes, but
also the capitalists, whose incomes are diminished, for,
if wages are increased, a smaller share will probably be
left as the reward of capital.   We must, of course,
as far as we can, consider the happiness of all concerned, remembering, however, that the working-
classes form the majority of the population and
capitalists only a small fraction.   The general result
of high wages would seem to be, in spite of the immense fortunes of American millionaires, an approach
to equality of wealth.   This would promote happiness,
for, while it would make happier the lower classes

raised to moderate competence from the starvation limit, it would less affect the richer classes, since they would merely have to diminish the amount of their luxuries, and custom would easily reconcile them to the change, particularly when they saw their friends and associates and all belonging to their class forced to make the same curtailment of their superfluous expenditure. Further, if there were perfect equality of wealth, the world would be spared from the pain of being poorer than others and from the happiness of being richer than others. As men are more inclined to compare themselves with those more fortunate than with those more miserable than themselves, inequality produces more pain than pleasure from comparison. Therefore a condition of equality is productive of happiness, and high wages as tending to such equality should be promoted by the efforts of every utilitarian.

Is it then possible to increase by human effort the reward of labour, and if so by what means? We have seen that trades unionism and strikes do something in this direction, as they prevent capitalists from venturing to give labourers very low wages when profits are very high. But more than this is wanted. The labourer wishes to secure for himself a larger fraction of the profits of production than he now gets. This could only be effected by strikes, if they were extended by a universal agreement of working men over the whole earth. Such an extensive agreement being impossible as far as we can see, some other means must be sought, and we naturally turn to the advocates of the nationalization of land, who are confident that they have in their scheme the true remedy for the poverty of the labouring world. They propose that the state should either buy, or confiscate all land, or impose upon rents such a high tax as would amount to practical confiscation. It is hard to see how the

position of affairs would be materially altered by
the state *buying* the land from the present holders.
The income of the state would, of course, be immensely increased by the rental of all the land, but
there could be no diminution of taxation, as interest,
about equal to the rent collected, would have to be
paid on the money borrowed by the state to
compensate the landowners. The proposal to *confiscate* landed property would, if carried out, have
much more far-reaching results. Mr. Henry George,
because direct confiscation would largely increase
the duties of government and would be a needless
shock to present habits of thought, would prefer
to do the confiscation indirectly by taxing the rent
of land so heavily that the landlords would only
have left them a small percentage to reward them
for the trouble of collecting rents, if they chose to
retain their property on such terms. This measure
would, he thinks, eradicate the curse of poverty
from modern civilisation, by enabling all labourers
to earn abundant wages free of all diminution by
taxation and would give government an overflowing
revenue, which would increase year by year, as the
material progress due to the new state of things
increased the rent of land. " This revenue arising
from the common property could be applied to the
common benefit, as were the revenues of Sparta.
We might not establish public tables—they would
be unnecessary ; but we could establish public baths,
museums, libraries, gardens, lecture rooms, music and
dancing halls, theatres, universities, technical schools,
shooting galleries, play-grounds, gymnasiums, &c.
Heat, light and motive power as well as water
might be conducted through our streets at public
expense ; our roads be lined with fruit trees ; dis-
coverers and inventors rewarded, scientific inves-
tigations supported ; and in a thousand ways the

public revenues made to foster efforts for the public benefit."

Such are the results promised from either the confiscation of all landed property by the state, or the substitution of one tax on rents for all the complicated systems of many taxes now in existence. The most important blessing promised in all this picture of the world's happiness in Mr. George's millennium is the increase of the labourers' wages. If this could really be secured to the extent he imagines, if, by enriching the community at the expense of the landlords, every labouring man could be assured of abundant wages, the utilitarian would be bound to support the scheme. For, in comparison with the banishment of extreme poverty and starvation from the world, the pain suffered by landlords deprived of their superfluous wealth would weigh lightly in the balance. Nor would the sufferings of landlords be as great as might at first sight be supposed. It is only proposed to confiscate land and the rent of land, not improvements added to the land in the shape of buildings. Thus a large part of the wealth of land owners would be untouched, and, as most of them are wealthy men, they could afford the loss of the mere rent of their land without being reduced to absolute poverty, unless their properties were heavily mortgaged. The capital left in their hands would be increased in value, being, like labour, entirely free from taxation, and the increase to the value of their capital would partially compensate them for the loss of rent. Peasant proprietors would gain more than they lost in rent, if the change brought them higher wages and more profits from their capital. In particular cases, such as poor widows, who derived a small income from land, special provision would, no doubt, be made to prevent them from becoming entirely de-

stitute.   Beside the   pain   of having   their wealth
diminished, landowners would also suffer much from
a feeling of injustice at the violation of their rights
of property.   But perhaps their indignation would
not be productive of as much pain as is now felt
by the vast number of indigent labourers, and still
more indigent unemployed who compare their want
with the luxury and abundant wealth of rich landowners, enjoying all the good things of the world
without toil.   This indignation is heightened by
the fact that property in land stands on a different
footing from other property, inasmuch as it was
originally for the most part obtained by confiscation,
and has risen to its present value not by the
labours of landowners, but by increase of production
due to mechanical inventions and freer trade, and by
consequent increase of population which tends to
make land scarcer and scarcer, and therefore more
and more valuable every year.

After a careful survey of all these considerations
the utilitarian would probably feel himself bound
to support the confiscation of the whole, or the
greater part of the land value of the country by
the state, if only it could be shown to increase wages
to the extent imagined by Mr. George and those
who think with him.   But here is the question on
which all depends.   Would the transference to the state
of all the wealth now derived from land permanently
raise the rate of wages and permanently afford
employment for everybody?   There is every reason
to believe that, if the state took to itself the
whole or nearly the whole of the rent of the
country, this one simple and easily collected tax would
render all other taxes unnecessary.   It would thus free
labour and capital from all taxation.   The capitalist
would not have to pay part of his earnings to the state
in the form of income tax, and the labourer and

capitalist alike would be able to buy the necessaries and luxuries of life, and the machines and tools which are the instruments of production at prices far lower than is now possible. For at present the consumer pays in the price of most of the articles he buys an indirect tax to the state. Under these circumstances the rewards of production to be divided between the capitalist and the labourer would be much increased, and the labourer would for a time be able to insist on getting his fair share of the increase. If capitalists refused to give higher wages, they would be compelled to do so by strikes; and, as they could yield to the strikes in this case without carrying on business unprofitably, they would yield. Thus the immediate result of the change would be great gain to labourers and capitalists at the expense of landowners. As most landowners are rich and nearly all labourers are poor, the change would be in the direction of equality which is itself a source of happiness, in addition to the immense diminution of misery in the millions of working men who are now underpaid and unemployed, but would then be working for abundant wages. But it is to be feared that the change for the better would only be temporary, like that produced by free trade or improvement in mechanical invention. A great impetus would be given to production partly by the impoverishment of the class which now most abundantly indulges in unproductive consumption. This increase of production would give the world a larger dividend of all things, especially of food and clothing and other necessaries of life, from which poor and rich, and especially the poor, would receive a greater share. But this happy state of affairs could not continue long. The population would soon rise in proportion to the increased supply of the means of subsistence, and then the competition of labourers would recommence as keenly as ever, and force down wages to their present average rate. To secure a temporary rise of wages, it would not appear to be justifiable from a utilitarian point of view to make such an immense interference with property, as the confiscation of all property in land or the one heavy tax on rents proposed by Mr. George would be. But it is clear that the benefit could only be temporary, unless the population doctrine of Malthus is false. This is clearly seen by Mr. George, who therefore devotes a large amount of space to the refutation of Malthus, attempting to show that the increase of population only drives wages down to a starvation point, because landlords are enabled by that increase to absorb more and more of the proceeds of labour in the form of rent. The arguments by which he attempts to prove that "in any given state of civilisation a greater number of people can collectively be better provided for than a smaller," and that "the new mouths which an increasing population calls into existence require no more food than the old ones, while the hands they bring with them can in the natural order of things produce more," are not strong enough to shake the Malthusian position. Therefore the benefit offered by his proposed remedy for poverty would only be temporary, and would be too dearly purchased by the disturbance of the security of all property, bitter feelings and civil wars, that would be sure to result from the attempt to transfer landed property without compensation from its present owners to the state.

Is there then no other remedy for low wages? One is suggested by what, as we have seen, would happen, if strikes for very high wages were made all over one particular country. In this case, much capital will leave the country, fewer labourers will be employed, and until the population is reduced to the limit suited to the new state of affairs, a very painful period of starvation will intervene, but after that painful interval high wages might be maintained. Why not, then, avoid this painful process by inverting the order of cause and effect and beginning with reduction of the population? If the labourers of England, by prudence and late marriages, reduced the number of their offspring by one half, the next generation would secure much higher wages. Of course another condition would be necessary to secure this result. Strict laws would have to be passed to prevent the immigration of foreign labourers. With these two conditions fulfilled, the supply of labour would be diminished and wages would rise high. The production of the country would be much diminished, as it would only be possible for capitalists to engage profitably in industries for which England has peculiar advantages, for instance, in mines and land of exceptional productiveness and of peculiarly advantageous situation. The self-denial necessary to bring about the required partial depopulation of England would involve a certain amount of pain, but much less than the starvation that would result from partial depopulation due to a general strike for higher wages. But it is hardly likely that the labouring classes will ever be taught to practise this kind of self-denial to any great extent. To postpone marriage, not for one's own inclination, but because one's early marriage inflicts infinitesimal disadvantage on the next generation of labouring men requires an amount of public spirit that will perhaps never be generally diffused through the world. Yet this is, according to Mill, the only means by which wages can be permanently improved, and the condition of the labourer be substantially ameliorated.

There does, however, seem to be another way in which the same object might be effected to a certain extent. Education increases the intelligence of working men. This increased intelligence may be expected to better their position in more ways than one. In the first place, it will teach them prudence in marriage, and so prevent them from increasing their number too rapidly, whenever a new invention increases the productive powers of the country. The advantage thus obtained, as it operates by limiting the supply of labourers, is only a means to the remedy the efficacy of which is admitted by Mill. Education, however, seems to work favourably in other ways. It is likely to increase the rapidity of productive invention, and so enable labourers to get larger wages without being forced to reduce their numbers. The increased intelligence produced by education will also teach them how to join their savings together as capital, and so be at once capitalists and labourers to the great advantage of their incomes. It will also enable them more clearly to estimate probabilities and to adjust their expenditure to their income. Indeed, the mere knowledge of arithmetic ought to be of great service to the working classes by helping them to determine when a strike is likely to be successful and when it would be suicidal folly. The settlement of this question is mostly a question of figures determining whether capitalists are or are not securing too high profits. In smaller matters too, the knowledge of figures will be of great use. It will enable the working man to settle better the many questions of domestic life, as to the advisability of marriage, change of place, or change of employment. In all these ways education will tend to give the labouring man a larger income, and will also teach him how to use that larger income to the best advantage.

It is generally assumed in newspapers and in the speeches of politicians that heavy taxation is an evil, and that the diminution of taxation is productive of happiness. The argument on which this conclusion is based is, that diminution of taxation increases the national wealth, and that each individual of the nation is likely to be benefited by that increase. Sometimes, however, diminution of taxation, instead of increasing national wealth, may actually diminish it. If the diminution of taxation diminishes a nation's army, navy, or police, below the quantity necessary for the security of life and property, the individual is likely to suffer, on the average, more from war and robbery, than he gained by relief from taxation. Diminution of taxation with such results would be advocated by no one but robbers or national enemies, and may, therefore, be left out of consideration. Those who desire diminution of taxation do so on the supposition that it may be secured by skilful economy, without impairing the efficiency of the defensive forces, or dangerously curtailing any other expenditure productive of national prosperity. This has, of course, often been done in the past. It has often happened, especially when taxes have been farmed out, that far more has been taken out of the taxpayer than finds its way to the national exchequer. Sometimes this is due to peculation on the part of the tax collectors, sometimes to the nature of the tax which cannot be levied without an excessive number of salaried collectors. In other cases, the waste comes later, and consists of extravagant expenditure of the proceeds of taxation. For instance, it is contended, rightly or wrongly, by Lord Randolph Churchill, and others, that the United Kingdom might have an equally or more efficient army at a less cost. Under such circumstances, the burden of taxation may be reduced without injury to the national wealth, or even, in many cases, with such a great addition to it as was effected by the repeal of the Corn Laws. Conversely heavy taxation may, and generally does, seriously diminish a nation's wealth. The partial depopulation of the once populous regions now included in the Turkish empire is no doubt, in a great measure, due to heavy taxation, and shows how injuriously heavy taxation may affect national wealth. But, if all taxes in the Turkish empire were remitted for ever,

H

the result would only be a temporary increase of happiness, owing to a temporary lightening of the struggle for existence. Very soon the population would rise in proportion to the remission of taxation, until the average income of the people became about what it was before. Owing to this increase of population which may generally be expected to follow increase of national wealth, lightening of taxation need not be expected to make the average man permanently wealthier, or less poor, than he was before. When the reform of taxation leads to increased wealth, and thereby to increased population, it does so by increasing production, much in the same way as improvement in machinery does, and has the same effect, or want of effect, upon the general happiness, as material progress.

In another way, however, reform in taxation may promote happiness. Some taxes tempt men to immoral conduct. As the assessment of the income tax to a large extent depends upon a man's own statement of his income, it rewards falsehood and dishonesty and punishes conscientiousness. In like manner heavy duties on imported goods encourage the kind of dishonesty called smuggling, which often leads to murder and other crimes. Even moderate duties tempt men, otherwise honourable, to condescend to all kinds of evasion, and to tell lies, in order to bring foreign goods in without paying the tax imposed by law. Unscrupulous men, to effect their object, try to bribe custom-house officials, who are often not firm enough to resist the temptation, and betray their trust to the ruin of their moral character. The farming out of taxes enriches generally the most unscrupulous speculators. Wherever, as in the above instances, taxation tempts men to commit vicious actions, its reform is desirable in the interests of happiness, as immoral conduct is in a high degree destructive of happiness.

Unjust taxes, as also all unjust laws, are very prejudicial to happiness. But what taxes or laws are unjust? If, adopting what may perhaps be called the natural utilitarian modification of the meaning of justice, we call all laws unjust which distribute privileges and burdens in a way productive of misery, then it is a verbal proposition to say that unjust laws produce misery, and it would be enough merely to determine which laws are just and which are unjust. Without attempting to settle exhaustively this question, so as to determine difficult questions about the justice or injustice of particular taxes, for and against which much may be said, let us consider certain old taxes admitted to be unjust on all sides except by those who were benefited by their imposition, and see whether they did much to diminish happiness. In Mahometan countries the levying of double taxes on Christians could not appear just to any except some Mahometans whose discrimination between right and wrong was blinded by fanaticism and the wish to have the burden of taxation thrust upon other shoulders. The injustice of this arrangement of taxation consisted in its imposing unequal burdens on men of equal wealth. Equally unjust in another way was the poll-tax of one shilling on every person above the age of sixteen imposed in England in the reign of Richard II. This law exacted as much from the poor as the rich, and its natural consequence was the rebellion of Wat Tyler, at the end of which, after the destruction of much private property, fifteen hundred persons were executed on the gibbet. Such unjust taxes as those just mentioned must be very injurious to happiness, from the bitter indignation excited in the minds of the sufferers and the division of the people into favoured and oppressed, who, instead of sympathising with each other, are animated by envy or proud contempt, according as they belong to the former or latter class. When the oppressed are carried away by their spirit of indignation, they break out in insurrection, which, whether successful or unsuccessful, is sure to be productive of much misery. In Europe, since the French Revolution, such modes of taxation as were flagrantly unjust have been for the most part swept away, to the great advantage of the general happiness. But if these unjust laws had never been imposed, or could have been abolished without insurrection and bloodshed, the improved state of affairs, which the leaders of the French Revolution were mainly instrumental in producing, might have been secured without the sufferings that necessarily accompany a violent uprising. The abuses of taxation are not now in modern Europe as they were before that cataclysm. Such taxes as are now vehemently condemned as unjust by socialists would in the past have almost entirely escaped criticism, or even been lauded as patterns of justice. The effect upon happiness of reform of taxation in a socialistic direction has been discussed above.

Before concluding this short survey of taxation from a utilitarian point of view, there is one principle which must never be forgotten. It is that almost all change of taxation has a tendency to diminish happiness. An old established, heavy tax presses less heavily both upon sellers and buyers than a light one newly imposed. In spite of the heavy taxes levied upon imported wine and spirits, wine merchants and hotel-keepers are as able to support themselves and their families as other tradesmen who deal in articles less heavily taxed. This is because they fix the price of wine and spirits at such a high price as reimburses them for the heavy taxes they pay, and the number of those who engage in these trades is so limited by calculations of prudence on the part of those choosing their calling in life that no more persons enter them than can expect a

fair profit out of the comparatively limited amount
of wine and spirits likely to be purchased at the
high prices necessitated by the heavy tax. On the
other hand buyers are so accustomed to the idea
of paying high prices for wine and spirits that they
look upon it as a matter of course and forbear to
be indignant. Suppose now that in England the
heavy tax on beer and spirits were taken off and
its place were partially supplied by a large increase
of the duty on tea. In this case the tea drinkers
would be annoyed at having to pay more for their
tea than they used to pay, but owing to the per-
verseness of human nature the drinkers of strong
drinks would not feel correspondingly thankful for
the diminution of the expense of their drink, so
that there would be a diminution of happiness equal
to the difference between the great pain of discontent felt
by the tea drinkers and the slight pleasure of gratification that the drinkers of alcohol would derive from buying
cheaper. Further, owing to the change in the
taxation, less tea and more alcoholic drink will be
consumed, and, therefore, a certain number of the
less prosperous wine merchants and innkeepers will
have either to change their trade or be ruined, or,
perhaps, do both, for it is often a ruinous measure
for a tradesman to give up his old trade and begin
life afresh.

On these grounds taxation should not be changed
except for the sake of such very solid advantage
to happiness as may be enough to counterbalance
the evil effects due to the mere fact of change.

CHAPTER VIII.

No doubt a great effect may be produced on happiness by alteration of domestic and social customs. Should polygamy be established all over the world, or are there some nations and climes in which polygamy and polyandry are preferable? Is early marriage or late marriage more productive of happiness? Should a man or boy choose his own wife, or a woman or girl her own husband, or should marriages be arranged by the parents of the principals? Should divorce and re-marriage be sanctioned by society? Should women be as free as the American girl of the period, or closely confined in the walls of a zenana, as in many parts of India, in Turkey, and in ancient Greece during the historic period? Ought they to be educated as men are, or differently, or not at all? Should men be allowed to choose their own calling, or be forced by a rigid system of caste to adopt that of their father and father's father? Is it better to dine at nine in the morning, as the ancient Normans did, and take supper at four or five in the afternoon, or to dine in the afternoon as they did in the days of William of Orange and George I., or to follow the fashion of the rich of to-day and dine late at night? Is it better to enjoy the social cup at meals as in Europe, or between meals as in America, or \on no occasion?\ Many such social questions present themselves for consideration, the settlement of which must be important for the utilitarian.

In the case of some of them it is possible to give a decided answer. We may safely assert that among the domestic customs most destructive of happiness the oriental custom of secluding women must take ~~almost~~ the foremost place. To abolish it gradually among the millions of people among whom it prevails would undoubtedly increase the average happiness or diminish the average misery of the world. The influence of the Mahometan religion has done much to intensify this evil. The natives of India trace its introduction into their country to the Mahometan conquest; at which date they say they began to seclude their women, partly in imitation of their conquerors, and partly in order to defend their wives and daughters from outrage. But the custom existed long before the Mahometan era, and not only in Asia but also in Eastern Europe among the most refined people of the ancient world. In fact it seems to be about as old as civilisation; but not older, for the great epics of Greece and India show that in the uncivilised period, when warriors fought habitually with stones and had hardly given up the idea of eating their conquered enemies, women enjoyed plenty of freedom of action. This fact makes the possibility of reform easier, as reform under the circumstances being a reversion to an earlier custom, can be advocated on conservative grounds and can not be regarded as a revolutionary destruction of a practice observed from time immemorial.

The infelicific effects of seclusion can hardly be disputed, though like all wide-spread customs its evil effects are softened by habituation. Oriental women, owing to the habitual seclusion of themselves and their ancestors through many generations, have come to hug their chains. Like canary birds they would not know how to use their liberty properly, if they were suddenly freed from their restrictions. But this is no reason why the gradual restoration of their freedom, accompanied by an improvement in education to fit them for their new position, should not be a great benefit not only to the women themselves but also to the society of which they form a part.

The clearest evil effect of seclusion is upon health. Human beings cannot expect to be healthy without a fair allowance of exercise and fresh air. But this is what oriental women cannot get, condemned as they are to spend the greater part of their life indoors. A small proportion of them may have access to private gardens and enjoy a certain amount of what is by a misnomer sometimes called carriage exercise. But a promenade in a small high-walled garden or a drive is a poor substitute for riding, or tennis, or walks in the open country. Even when driving they get little fresh air owing to the thick veil with which they are shrouded. And after all, it is only the small minority of the rich that can afford private gardens or carriages. Most of them are shut up in small crowded rooms, from which they seldom or never emerge. Strong vigorous health must be all but impossible under such conditions. Then it must be remembered that it is not only the women themselves who suffer from seclusion. Their children succeed to their weakness. When one half of the parents of a race are deprived of the possibility of vigorous health, it is no wonder if each succeeding generation is less healthy than its predecessor.

The oriental defence of the system we are considering is that it is necessary for the preservation of female chastity. Put into a utilitarian form the argument would be that seclusion secures chastity, and that unchastity is so productive of misery that it is reasonable to secure chastity at the expense of all the unhealthiness due to seclusion. Now, in the absence of experience to the contrary, it might have been supposed that seclusion is a safeguard of chastity and that liberty has the opposite effect. But there is an overwhelming

?. Indeed!

amount of experience to the contrary in the fact that
European and ~~even~~ American women are certainly as
virtuous as their sisters in the east. There seems no
reasonable ground for doubting this fact. At first
sight the large number of divorce cases chronicled in
English newspapers would seem to point to an opposite
conclusion, as compared with the infrequency of such cases
in the history of oriental families. But the reason of
this difference is not the superior chastity of women in
the east, but the oriental custom of settling such matters
by the family or caste without appealing to the law.
The aberrations from virtue that in England lead to
divorce cases do not as a rule in the east appear in the
newspapers in the records of judicial cases, unless they
are revenged by murder, and not always even then, although in the newspapers of the east there is no lack of
murders actuated by jealousy. As experience shows that
women are just as capable of being virtuous in a state of
liberty as when subjected to jealous confinement, and
that the variety of interests that occupy the mind of a
free woman with plenty of liberty of action is a better
preservative against error than stone walls and doors,
the seclusion of women must, if justified at all, find
some other defence.

Can it be defended, on Darwinian grounds, against
the charge of being injurious to health? No doubt,
if all over the world owing to some universal law of
nature the whole of the human race or all the women
were compelled to live in houses without ever emerg-
ing into the open air, human nature would be able
gradually to adapt itself to its environment, and
those unable to live and be healthy without fresh air
and outdoor exercise, or without their wives and
daughters enjoying fresh air and outdoor exercise,
would die out and leave no descendants. Thus there
would be left to people the world, only those fitted
by hereditary temperament to be healthy and happy

indoors. But there is no such law of nature, and consequently nations and families who seclude their women are heavily handicapped in the struggle for existence with those who live a life which, in the present condition of things, is healthier. Even in oriental countries like India the poor cannot seclude their wives and daughters, and might be expected, in the long run, to rise successfully against the rich, and by superior bodily health and strength due to a more rational life would overthrow those, who before by their power and wealth were able to follow the pernicious practice of seclusion of women. This was pretty clearly shown by the rise of the poor un-civilised Marathas against their Mahometan rulers. Had it not been for the British conquest, they would doubtless have become the rulers of India, but only for a time, until having adopted from the conquered the practice of seclusion, and being able by their wealth to keep it up, they had paved the way for their own physical deterioration. The weakening effects of this practice partly explains also the rapid fall of many oriental empires when attacked by poor and hardy mountaineers, and especially the deterioration that Mahometan nations seem to suffer from prosperity. The Arabs, and after them the Turks, on first adopting Mahometanism, dis-played an immense amount of energy and valour, but in both cases after a few generations these qualities disappeared or remained only among the poorer classes who had not sufficient means to seclude their women. It would therefore appear that though, in the long course of ages, portions of the human race, if isolated from the rest of the world, might manage to be healthy although secluding their women, yet this slower process has always been cut short by the more rapid disappearance of in-dividuals, families, and nations following this practice and having to contend in the struggle for existence with ordinary men who are the offspring of mothers whose minds and limbs have not been cramped by seclusion. This being the case, one may be tempted to argue in favour of seclusion that it is not likely to damage much the happiness of the human race, as those who follow the practice, tend to die out, and, like suicides, leave few or no descendants. But unfortunately, besides the fact that this dying out involves a large amount of painful ill-health and killing, the practice has such attractions to the oriental mind, that many of those, who take the place of the individuals, families, and communities that have died out owing to seclusion, soon adopt the same bad custom, which they are enabled to do owing to the wealth they have won at the expense of the displaced. So that the custom remains, however much those who practise it suffer in health and lose the happiness that good health confers.

And even if seclusion of women were as compatible with health as their liberty, the practice should still be eschewed by utilitarians as directly diminishing the happiness of women. It is only after long confinement that women come to hug their chains and prefer confinement to liberty. Naturally as they grow up they miss the freedom they enjoyed as little girls. Nor are they prepared for seclusion by heredity, for their male parents have been accustomed to liberty, and women derive their mental characteristics as much from their fathers as their mothers. Thus seclusion would seem to diminish happiness both indirectly by militating against health, and also directly. Therefore oriental utilitarians have a great work to do in effecting by precept and example the gradual extinction of this custom.

Another oriental custom, that affords scope to utilitarian effort, is early marriage. This custom is the rule, though not without exceptions, among the two hundred and fifty million inhabitants of India. A large number of those sections of the Indian com-

munity, which marry young, aggravate the evil results
of the practice by prohibiting widows from re-
marriage, and subjecting them to social tyranny.
Indian widows are regarded as degraded beings, who
have lost their husbands owing to misdemeanours
committed in one of their lives, and their presence
is supposed to be ominous of evil. They are compelled to shave their hair, forego the use of ornaments,
eat the coarsest food, and take the lowest place in
the household hierarchy. Owing to early marriage
and the prevention of widow re-marriage, there are a
disproportionate amount of widows in India. In
England, only the death of men produces widows; in
India, nearly every boy that dies leaves a widow
behind him, and by the prohibition of re-marriage
most of those who are once made widows remain widows
for ever. In India, there are out of a population of
254,000,000 more than 23,000,000 widows. India, with
ten times the population of England and Wales, has
twenty - three times the number of widows. The
position of widows is proverbially unhappy all over
the world. In Christian countries, their unhappy
state is alleviated by the religious sanction supporting
with all its power the duty of kindness and justice
to women and children bereft of their natural pro-
tectors, as among the most sacred of moral duties.
Hindu religion and custom, on the contrary, as we
have seen, goes out of its way to intensify the bitterness of the widow's lot. Thus in India, widows are
not only more numerous, but also more miserable
than in the rest of the world. Also early marriage
helps to make the average state of the widow exceptionally unhappy. In England, few women become
widows until they have passed the prime of
youth and the most passionate age of life. In India,
a vast majority of widows are young girls, whose
passions are too strong to be controlled by reason,

and, as a natural consequence, they are not unlikely to fall away into vice and misery.

It may be answered that in Europe, there are not only widows, but also a large number of women who remain unmarried till their death, while in India almost every woman gets married, and old maids are scarcely ever heard of. In England and Wales in 1881, there were out of a population of 26,000,000, only 1,000,000 widows, but of unmarried women above the age of twenty, there were nearly 2,000,000. This, however, is a very partial answer. The unhappiness of European spinsters should on the average be much less than that of Indian widows. As marriage in Europe depends mainly on a woman's own free will, almost any woman can marry, if she is very anxious to do so. Consequently, a large proportion of European spinsters are women either totally averse to married life, or who are not very anxious for matrimony, and therefore have been disinclined to accept such men as have happened to ask for their hands. Thus, there is good reason to believe that English spinsters are less dissatisfied with their state than Indian widows. Further, owing to early marriage, Indian wives and husbands are more likely to be dissatisfied with each other than English wives and husbands. Of course, such generalisations are subject to exceptions. Many English wives and husbands, after a few years or months of married life, find their tempers incompatible. But such unfortunate too late discoveries are less likely to be made in the case of husbands and wives who have chosen each other after arriving at years of discretion, than when a match has been made probably on prudential considerations by the parents of bride and bridegroom.

Early marriage is also said to be bad from a physiological point of view, as being injurious to the health both of parents and children, on which account

Plato in his Republic does not allow his guardians to marry before the age of twenty-five, and then, only to women of twenty years old and upwards. Thus, on the score of health, and as much happiness as depends upon health, there is the same objection to early marriage as to the seclusion of women.

But it is unnecessary to dwell upon the evils of early marriage and enforced widowhood, as they have been detailed so exhaustively in the writings of Mr. Malabari, a Parsee of Bombay, who, in a true utilitarian spirit, has devoted himself heart and soul to their extinction in India. The effect produced by his enthusiasm and literary labours in this field is somewhat marred by the fact that the Hindus rather resent being lectured upon their manners and customs by a Parsee or any other outsider. More result may be expected from the efforts of enlightened members of the Hindu community, if only they do not urge on the wheel of progress so rapidly as to provoke reaction. *Festina lente* should be their motto. If all educated Hindus would take up the good cause with the same enthusiasm and self sacrifice as Mr. Malabari, and with such knowledge of the dangers and difficulties in the way of reform as can only be possessed by a Hindu, the happiness of millions would be increased, and, as this increased happiness to India would not be obtained at the expense of any other portion of the human race, general happiness would thereby be promoted.

Closely connected with the seclusion of women, early marriage, and the prohibition of widow re-marriage is the question of caste, because it is by the tyranny of caste rules that these practices are enforced upon the majority of Hindus. Therefore, the evil effects of these practices are arguments against caste. But caste is far more wide-reaching in its results, and rules with a rod of iron the lives of men, as well as of women and children. Its great effect is to sub-divide India into small communities of men who can have no social intercourse with each other. It is therefore condemned by those who have studied the institution, as hostile to the spread of sympathy between man and man. " Caste," says Mr. Sherring, is "a sworn enemy to human happiness. Laws, customs, social compacts, and the sweet acts of self-denial so frequently practised between man and man, are intended to promote the welfare of mankind, to increase the sum of human joy, to make homes tranquil, and to strengthen all the ties by which one family is bound to another. Caste was instituted for a different purpose. It seeks to sever natural ties, to alienate friends, to harden the heart, to stifle sympathy, to increase pride and self-esteem, to generate misanthropy, to repress the kindly affections, and to destroy mutual confidence and trust, without which society is beset with stings, and becomes a stranger to genuine comfort and peace."

This may seem an exaggerated indictment to those who have not realised the immense number of castes in India, and the strict social exclusiveness which separates each caste from the rest of the world. In ancient Persia there are said to have been only four castes, priests, soldiers, husbandmen, and tradesmen. In ancient Egypt there were, according to Herodotus, seven castes, priests, soldiers, cowherds, swineherds, tradesmen, interpreters, and boatmen. But how far these Persian and Egyptian castes were sub-divided, and how strict were the lines of separation, we know very imperfectly, except that it is stated, that in Egypt the swineherd was looked down upon as a degraded being, and was not allowed to enter the temples. It is to India where the caste system is still in full force that one must look for experience of its working. It is very commonly supposed, that in India there are only four castes—(1) The Brahmins or priestly caste, (2) The Kshatryas or military caste, (3) The Vaishyas or mercantile caste, (4) The Shudras or servile caste. If there were only these four castes in India, the accusation that caste restrains sympathy within narrow limits would have less force, for there is plenty of room for the exercise of sympathy for those who can have intimate friendly intercourse with even a fourth part of their fellow-men in a thickly populated country like India. But in truth, this fourfold division is only the original starting-point of the caste system. When the Hindus first divided themselves into these four castes, the barrier of exclusiveness does not appear to have been so strict as it has since become, and men and women of different castes married one another. From the offspring of these mixed marriages new castes have arisen, until now the number of castes is astonishingly large. In the census for 1881, over nineteen thousand caste names were given in to the census officers. This shows the immense number of Indian castes, even allowing for the probability that, in many cases, different caste names were given in by different individuals of the same caste. So firmly fixed is the caste system in India, that even the native Christians are divided into castes. When such an immense number of divisions supplements the ordinary divisions of society according to place and wealth, the Hindu must often have very few human beings with whom to associate in friendly sympathy. Think of a Hindu in his village or town. Like other men he depends for society upon his near neighbours, and especially upon those who are neither much richer, nor much poorer, than himself. But by caste rules he is still further limited in the circle of his possible friendships. He can only familiarly associate with those of his neighbours of about the same fortune as himself, who happen also to belong to the same caste. With those who belong to any one of the thousands of other castes he cannot, as a rule, join in a social meal, or form a marriage connection. Even without such restrictions it is often hard enough for men to find a sufficient number of congenial friends among their neighbours. Just as friendship adds much to human happiness, any institution which, like caste, limits a man's power of selecting congenial friends must be prejudicial to happiness.

Even members of the same caste are restricted in their social intercourse. The men take their meals first, and afterwards the women by themselves. Conversation is forbidden at the time of eating. By the rules which regulate the Namburi Brahmins it is decreed that the "Brahmani woman is strictly prohibited from having access to or seeing any other man besides her lawful husband, and likewise her own male children are restricted from having access to her after they have attained the age of fourteen years." Thus caste like slavery may bring about a forcible separation between mother and child.

We have seen reason to believe that equality is productive of happiness. Caste in one of its principal aspects resembles slavery by being a contravention of the equality of men. An immense number of the regulations of caste are intended to make a great gulf of separation between Brahmins and the rest of mankind. The contempt of white slave-master for black slave, or of Greek for barbarian was much less arrogant than the contempt with which the Brahmin is taught to look down upon the lower castes. "Indian caste," says Dr. Wilson, "is the condensation of all the pride, jealousy, and tyranny of an ancient and predominant people dealing with the tribes which they have subjected, and over which they have ruled often without the sympathies of a recognised common humanity." As Dr. Wilson was a missionary, his judgment on the subject might be naturally suspected, if it were not abundantly supported by extracts from the sacred books of the Hindus. Brahmins and gods are sometimes coupled together in caste regulations. The law books say that in the house of a king, in a cow's fold, and in the presence of a god and Brahmin, and at the time of worship and eating, shoes ought to be pulled

I

off. "The Brahmins are earthly gods, to be adored and honoured with commendations," according to the Kalki Purana. In the Padma Purana it is written that "the Brahmin is the exalted lord of all the castes. To him should gifts be made with faith and reverence. The Brahmin represents all divinities in himself, a visible god on the earth, who saves the giver in the impassable ocean of the world," and again elsewhere in the same book we are told that "Whatever good man bows to a Brahmin, reverencing him as Vishnu, is blessed with long life, with sons, with renown, and with prosperity." In all ways, says Manu, Brahmins are to be worshipped; they are a supreme Divinity. Men of the servile class were only created for the purpose of serving Brahmins.

According to the same lawgiver a Brahmin may without hesitation take the property of a Shudra. The Namburi Brahmins are so proud that they will not allow Shudras to approach within three paces of them, and, if a Pulyar touch them, they must immediately bathe and change their Brahminical threads and clothes, and absolve themselves by reading the Vedas before they dare to enter their houses. The lower castes are compelled by the caste regulations to humiliating restrictions in their mode of life. The Chandala and Shoapaka must live outside towns, be denied the use of unbroken vessels, and have as their sole wealth dogs and asses. Their clothes must be those of the dead, their dishes broken pots, their ornaments rusty iron. Other classes must have no intercourse with them. The Brahmins and other castes are by no means to be equal in the sight of the law. If a Vaishya slanders a Brahmin he must be fined one hundred and fifty or two hundred panas; if a Brahmin slanders a Vaishya, he is fined twenty-five, and, if he slanders a Shudra, only twelve panas. A Shudra slandering a Brahmin must suffer corporal punishment.

Should a Brahmin kill a Shudra, he pays no more penance than if he killed a cat, an ichneumon, a frog, a lizard, an owl, or a crow; but a person intending to strike a Brahmin with intent to kill remains in hell a hundred years, and, if he actually strikes him, a thousand. Every drop of a Brahmin's blood shed and attracting particles of dust, demands a thousand years' torment for each of these particles. These instances, most of which, with many others to a similar effect, may be found in Dr. Wilson's posthumous work on "Indian Caste," illustrate the immense arrogance with which the Brahmin is taught by his sacred books to look down on his fellow-men. Nor is this relation of contempt on the one side and degrading inferiority on the other confined to the Brahmins and Shudras. All the castes are arranged in a kind of hierarchy, the higher members of which are taught to despise the lower, and, when they can, inflict upon them marks of inferiority. Thus the Shudras, though so far below the Brahmins, themselves lord it over the castes of inferior dignity. They are divided into many castes, and some of the higher caste Shudras consider themselves polluted by contact with lower caste Shudras. Below all the Shudras are ranked certain outcast and polluted castes who pay to the Shudras almost as much reverence as the Shudras pay the Brahmins. Such, for instance, are the Pulayars, who form one-twelfth of the whole population of Travancore, and must keep well out of the way of even the Shudras. In Mr. Mateer's account of native life in Travancore we read that "Until lately Pulayars were not allowed even to approach the roads. When they had palm-leaf umbrellas and other small articles to sell, they laid them down near the highway, and, standing at the appointed distance, shouted to their customers . . . Cottayam Pulayars put a few green twigs on the roadside, near where they are working, to warn

off high castes.   Pulayars, walking on the high road,
are required to run off into the jungles or fields when
high-caste people pass along.   Where there is plenty
of room, a kind of side-walk is sometimes formed in
this way.   It is most painful to see a poor and in-
offensive woman with a load on her back, or burdened
with an infant, scramble up the steep side of the road
and retire into the jungle, to allow a high-caste man
to pass."   In this account it must be remembered that
"high caste" includes Shudras as well as Brahmins.
It must not be supposed that such intolerable preten-
sions to superiority are submitted to without painful
feelings of bitter indignation among the oppressed
and degraded.   Buddhism was a great protest against
the tyranny of caste, and very nearly drove Brah-
minism out of India.   Its success showed the strength
of the feeling of indignation among the lower castes,
and the temporary nature of its success showed the
immense strength of the caste system, which, though
for a time overthrown, managed once more to recover
its ascendency so completely, that now Buddhism is
practically an extinct faith in India.

All the caste regulations given above, which draw
degrading distinctions between caste and caste, must
be condemned as terribly destructive of humility,
sympathy between man and man, compassion for
the weak, and, therefore, of happiness.   There are
also many other regulations in the caste codes which
will be condemned equally by the ordinary moralist and by the utilitarian.   Some of the caste regulations entail great inconvenience even on the castes
in whose favour they are made.   "All this super-
stitious punctiliousness," remarks Mr. Mateer in his
"Native Life in Travancore," "is fraught with
great inconvenience to the unenlightened high castes
themselves.   They are unable to travel by sea unless
they could land daily to cook and eat their food,

that prepared with the water on board ship being ceremonially unclean. When travelling by rail along with other classes, they dare not even take a draught of water to refresh themselves; and often there is great suffering from hunger when habitations belonging to their own caste are not at hand. A friend of ours calling a native doctor to the Hills for a serious emergency, the poor man could eat nothing but plantain fruits during the two days he was in patient and kindly attendance." In some exceptional cases the directions given to the castes seem directly opposed to ordinary morality, and, therefore, to happiness. For instance, according to Manu, a Brahmin must live by truth and falsehood rather than by hired service. But, on the whole, the principal objections that the utilitarian will have to the caste system will be on account of the degradation of the lower castes, the seclusion of women, early marriage, enforced widowhood and unkindness to widows.

The culmination of the evils sanctioned by caste is to be found in the practice of suttee. This rite, however, stands on a different footing from the other evils we have been considering, inasmuch as it is recommended as a counsel of perfection, not prescribed as necessary. It was, however, supposed to have such peculiar efficacy in securing a husband's salvation, that wives of the higher castes abstaining from it were liable to contempt and contumely. There were differences in the arrangements allowable according to the caste of the victim. Brahmin women were not allowed to sacrifice themselves except on their husband's dead body. Women of other high castes might and did do so after their husbands had been dead many years, when, perhaps, they found the life of widowhood intolerable. Some of the lowest castes seem to have been denied the honour and privilege of committing suttee in any form. The duty of suttee is not prescribed by Manu, but is advocated in the Brahma-purana and may be regarded as the natural result of the severe regulations by which widows are oppressed. It is not unnatural that, to avoid the evils of existence as a widow, a woman should make a virtue of necessity and die on her husband's funeral pyre. Here is a description of a case of suttee described by an eye-witness in a letter to the *Bombay Courier* of September 10th, 1802, which will illustrate how the ceremony was performed. " About two o'clock the body (of the husband) was brought to the pagoda feet foremost. The wife very richly dressed walked close to the head. At the pagoda some ceremonies were performed by the Brahmins, and the lady threw large quantities of the red powder, which is used at the Hooly, over every person near her, after which she with the corpse went down into the river which was close by, and, after bathing and throwing dust about for a long time, she followed the corpse to the pile, which was about three feet high. She then took off all her ornaments except her nut and two gold rings and distributed them among her mother and children. She gave a few rings to some other female relations who attended. None of the daughters or mother seemed really affected; they appeared to weep, but you might see they were inwardly pleased at the honour that would redound to their family from the victim's fortitude. After she had given away all her jewels, the Brahmins gave her sandal-wood dust which she distributed to all near her. She then walked round the pile, the Brahmins salaaming to her feet as she passed. When she arrived at the feet of the corpse which was the entrance (the wood having been piled about two feet at the head and about the height of the body as it lay), Roba (a Brahmin under whom the dead man had served) got up and went to her, knelt down and made salaam with his head to her feet, and complimented her on her virtue and fortitude, at which she smiled and seemed highly pleased. She then turned, and having salaamed to her husband's feet she entered the pile, and walking up to the head with a firm step she sat herself down and took the head of the corpse into her lap, where she remained perfectly composed whilst the Brahmin piled up the rest of the wood, putting great quantities of dry cow-dung round her person. The wood was laid in a triangular form, so that the entrance at the foot was never closed, and you saw the woman very plain. After it was finished and closed at the top, it looked like an oven. There were a great many pieces put over where she sat, which by very little exertion from without would have been thrown down upon her and crushed her to death, but there was no occasion for that to be done. A lighted torch was given her by an old Brahmin (who remained at the entrance of the pile) with which she very deliberately set fire to the cow-dung all round her, and sat surrounded by the flame without altering a feature. When the flame appeared at the top, the old Brahmin threw a handful of something full in her face which instantly caused a great blaze, and she was entirely enveloped in it. A band of country music then struck up, the Brahmins began knocking the upper part of the pile down upon the bodies, and every person present began clapping their hands and hollowing as loud as they could." The most painful feature in this account is the provision made by pieces of wood piled above her to prevent the victim from bursting away from the pile if her courage failed her at the last moment. When this happened, the poor women trying to escape were often crushed by the Brahmins under the wood of the pile, or, if they got out of the pile, were cut down with the sword.

Such scenes were of frequent occurrence at the commencement of the century, until suttee was placed by law on the same footing as murder by Lord Bentinck, who, in spite of the fact that he stamped out a custom dear to caste prejudices, is still remembered with affection by the people of India as one of the best of English Governor-generals. But much still requires to be done. Suttee being the natural result of the tyranny exercised by caste over the Hindu widow, it may seem from a utilitarian point of view an act of doubtful benevolence to prevent her from escaping her miseries by a voluntary and honoured death. What is required to supplement the abolition of suttee, is some measure for the amelioration of the widow's lot and her freedom from the indignities she is now subjected to on account of her supposed crimes. But this can hardly be effected by law. It may, however, be brought about gradually by the influence of education. This is recognised by one of the noblest champions of woman's rights in India, the Pandita Ramabai, who herself a widow has set about the work of educating widows in India and teaching them to learn to support themselves and be independent. As soon as Indian women have secured the full advantage of the education offered to the people of India, they will effect a reform of the customs that now press so unfairly on the weaker sex.

The utilitarian will prefer to reform the caste system by the gradual influence of education rather than attempt suddenly to subvert it, because the regulations of caste are not by any means all opposed to utilitarianism. In the codes that regulate the castes, there is mixed up with much that the utilitarian will condemn a large amount of good ordinary morality, the obedience to which must be productive of happiness.

A large number of the regulations are neither for nor against happiness. Such, for instance, is the rule that the stick with which a Brahmin rinses his teeth is to be twelve inches long, that of a Kshatriya is to be eleven, and that of a Shudra nine. But mixed up in strange confusion with such immaterial regulations are precepts in accordance with the ten commandments. Thus the Brahmin is commanded to abstain from honey, flesh, perfumes, garlands, vegetable juices, women, acidulated substances, the killing of animated beings, unguents for his limbs, black powder for his eyes, wearing sandals, using an umbrella, sensual desires, wrath, covetousness, dancing, singing, dice, detraction, and falsehood. He is warned by Manu against being puffed up by the lofty position given him in the hierarchy of castes, for " by falsehood, sacrifice becomes vain ; by pride, austerities go for nought ; by the dishonour of priests, life is diminished; and by the display of charity, its fruit is destroyed." Many of the regulations must have been originally prompted by utilitarian considerations of a sanitary character. Such are the rules for ablutions, for the protection of tanks from pollution, and the penalty imposed upon those who drink water or eat food that has fallen to the ground. Out of the long collections of regulations for the castes on all kinds of subjects in the sacred books a large body of prescriptions productive of happiness might be extracted, and in some cases where the letter of the laws is infelicific it is possible nevertheless to see that they have been dictated by a spirit of benevolence. It is likely that, with the progress of knowledge, the felicific regulations will gradually render obsolete those prejudicial to happiness. At present caste wields the overpowerful sanction of public opinion in support of its rules whether good or bad, and may be regarded as a rigid enforcer of a system of conduct which on the whole is pro-

ductive of happiness. If caste were suddenly overthrown, it is not unlikely that an immense number of
individuals who are now kept in order by the fear
of their castes would break out into all kinds of
licentiousness. This being the case, the sudden
destruction of caste would probably do far more harm
than good. Therefore the utilitarian will rather strive
to promote the reform of caste from within by education
and by giving more and more importance to those parts
of the caste regulations, which are in accordance with
general happiness, and obedience to which would be
found ultimately to be inconsistent with the proud
disdain of the higher castes, with the seclusion of
women, and with the cruel condition of widows.

Undoubtedly this internal process of reform has long
been going on steadily and silently. The view of caste
derived by Sanskrit scholars from the ancient literature
of India is a picture of caste in its extreme form, in the
form which the most conservative upholders of the
system would like to see restored, and is not literally
true of modern India. The authority of Manu as a
legislator is now practically obsolete, and many of his
regulations have become a dead letter, though their spirit
may be followed as far as the changed circumstances due
to the lapse of centuries allow. Also the picture given
by Mr. Mateer of caste in Travancore must not be supposed to be applicable to India generally. In and around
Bombay I have never had experience of anything ap-
proaching the spirit of contemptuous exclusiveness of
which he gives so many striking instances. The world
is moving even in the East, and the caste system has not
shown itself entirely incapable of that internal reform by
which alone old institutions can survive and adapt themselves to the changing spirit of successive ages.

CHAPTER IX.

A LARGE number of persons suppose that the happiness of the world would be immensely promoted by the general adoption of vegetarianism, and many of them have devoted much time and trouble to writing books and pamphlets in support of their view. They show clearly that the universal adoption of vegetarianism would enable the earth to support a much larger population. As to this part of their teaching there can be no doubt. If the pasture land now used for the support of sheep and oxen intended for the table were converted into corn land, the earth would produce food for a much greater amount of inhabitants than it can now support. It has been calculated that London alone consumes in the year 500,000 oxen, 2,000,000 sheep, 200,000 calves, and 300,000 swine. If the citizens who consume all these animals were converted suddenly to vegetarianism, they could out of the savings due to their conversion feed all the poor of London sumptuously every day. The same conclusion would be true of the whole world, in which at present there is much misery owing to want and starvation. If vegetarianism were adopted all over the world, there would be far more than enough food for the fourteen or fifteen hundred millions who now inhabit it.

Upon this indisputable fact the vegetarians by making a false assumption base a wrong conclusion. They suppose that, when they have shown this, they have proved that vegetarianism would drive want and starvation out of the world. This conclusion rests on the assumption that the adoption of vegetarianism would not affect the population of the world. But any such assumption is opposed to fact. In India and China and other countries where vegetarianism is the rule there is just as much of the misery of want as in carnivorous countries. This is because population increases in proportion to the supply of food, unless the increased supply of food is accompanied by increased prudence. But increased prudence may just as easily come into play without any increase of the food supply. So there is no reason to suppose that vegetarianism, by increasing the food supply, would save the human race from the pains of want. It would add a few additional millions to the population of the world, but increase of population in itself should not be promoted by any utilitarians except those who are confirmed optimists.

In fact, if we consider the matter aright, we shall probably come to the contrary conclusion, and see that the practice of eating flesh is really a useful defence against famine by providing nations with a kind of reserve fund in times of great scarcity. In countries like England where much flesh is eaten, the population can in bad years evade famine by abstaining to a certain extent from such costly food as beef and mutton; but in vegetarian countries this resource is not available, as the population is almost as large as the average produce of the country can possibly support, so that, if the produce falls below the average, it is terribly difficult to find any means of economy by which to avoid starvation. This is the principal reason why India and China suffer so much more from famine than European nations. In these countries the wages of the poorer labourers are about three pence a day, on which they can barely purchase the rice necessary to keep their bodies in working order. When a bad year comes and their vegetable food becomes dearer,

and their employers themselves suffering from the bad
times cut down their miserable wages still further or
are unable to pay them, the unfortunate men must
die in large numbers. Thus the very fact that animal
food is so much dearer than vegetable food is a utilitarian argument against the universal adoption of
vegetarianism.

A common argument in favour of vegetarianism is
that the eating of animal food necessitates a great deal
of cruelty in the shambles and in the chase. We have
seen that hunting does not on the whole diminish the
happiness of hunted animals. Nor does it appear that
death in the shambles is more painful than the natural
death of animals. In fact, even at present, it is less painful, and it might be rendered still more painless by the use
of chloroform or electricity. The diminution of pain, however, due to the suddenness of death at the shambles, is
about counterbalanced by the pain suffered by the animals when conveyed by train or driven by road to their
place of death. Sometimes at the end of their journey
their misery is aggravated by a source of pain rare in
the case of the lower animals. Sheep, certainly, when
they are being driven in to the shambles, often show distinctly by their terror that they have some idea of what
is going to happen to them, and anticipate death. On the
whole, according to present arrangements, the fact that
they are used as food cannot be seen to affect, one way
or another, the happiness of the lower animals. Therefore, as far as the happiness of the lower animals alone
is concerned, utilitarians should, instead of advocating
vegetarianism, rather exert themselves to diminish the
pains suffered by animals on their way to the slaughter-
house, and to render still less painful their death there,
which even under present arrangements is not so cruel as
the lingering death they would otherwise have to die.

If, then, the eating of animal food is to be condemned
by utilitarians on account of cruelty, it must be not on

account of suffering inflicted on the lower animals, but because it hardens the hearts of the men who eat and the men who kill sheep and oxen, and so diminishes their happiness, and, it may be added also, that of those with whom they come into contact. For men who are cruel to lower animals are likely also to be cruel to their fellow-men. The general belief in the brutalising effect produced on the mind by the butcher's trade is shown by the common though erroneous idea that butchers cannot serve on a jury, and by the frequency with which "butcher" is used as a term of reproach. On the other hand, there are, no doubt, many exceptions to these general tendencies. There are many butchers who are humane and kindly men, and the excesses committed by the Sepoy mutineers, together with other facts of oriental history, show that vegetarianism and tender regard for animals are no effectual defence against violent outbursts of cruelty against men. On the whole, however, we should be less inclined to expect gentleness and humanity in butchers than in any other trade or profession. Thus the general adoption of vegetarianism would save many thousands of men from entering a trade that is likely to brutalise their minds, and so make them unhappy themselves and the cause of unhappiness to others. This is the most distinct attraction that vegetarianism has to offer to the utilitarian. There is also to be considered the less marked but more extensive bad effect produced on those who eat animal food and see the carcasses of animals exposed in shop windows. However slightly each individual eater of animal food may impair his humane feeling, the aggregate impairment obtained by multiplying this slight impairment by the millions of men who eat flesh must be very great. Therefore the utilitarian ought to do all he can to support the vegetarian movement, if it were not for the fact mentioned above that vegetarian populations are peculiarly exposed to the ravages of famine.

These two considerations, that vegetarianism aggravates

famines, and that eating flesh tends to render less com-
passionate men generally, and one class of men in particular, may be supposed to balance each. Therefore the
utilitarian will neither advocate nor oppose vegetarianism,
but do his best to defend both vegetarians and flesh
eaters against the sources of pains to which they are
peculiarly exposed.

The great famines, to which vegetarian nations are
peculiarly exposed, are principally due to great variations
in the rain supply. A very barren country with little
variation in the produce year by year is much less liable to
famine than a rich country that suffers once in ten years
from droughts or destructive floods, because in the former
case the population is not likely to be much too large for
the yearly produce of the country, while in the latter case
the number of the population is determined by the large
amount of the produce during average good years, so that
it is far too great for the produce during the exceptional
year of drought. Hence, the best preventive of famines
is regularity in a country's annual production of wealth.
In agricultural countries, and all countries to a large
extent agricultural, this object is best secured by extensive irrigation, by which, when rains are deficient, the
deficiency is supplied by more extensive use of the great
rivers and lakes of a country. Much can be done by the
storage of water in tanks and other large reservoirs, such
as dammed-up rivers, in which a large supply of the abundant rainfall of good years may be kept for use in years
of drought. Another defence against extreme scarcity of
food in bad years is provided by facility of communication
between different parts of the world, so that the bad
effects of a deficient harvest in England may be
alleviated by abundant harvests in Russia, India, or
America, and *vice versa.* For it can hardly happen
that drought can prevail in the same year over all the
countries of the world. Facility of communication, it
should be observed, has a double operation in preventing

variation in the supply and cost of food from year to year, that is, in preventing the principal cause of famine. It tends to increase the price of corn in good years, and to diminish the price in bad years. In years of abundance a country in communication with the rest of the world can find a market for its superabundant produce in other countries where the harvest is less abundant. Thus, the farmers have not to sell their corn at such a low price as they would have been compelled to take, had they been confined to the market provided by their own country. Also, prices being only moderately low, and a large amount of the produce going to other countries, there is not such a stimulus given to increase of population in the country with the good harvest, and the labouring classes are not so likely on the strength of the exceptionally good harvest to exceed the number that an average year can support. In bad years, on the other hand, corn will be imported from the countries that have had a good harvest, and so the rise of prices that would otherwise have taken place will be diminished. Consequently, in two ways, the difference between the price of food in good and bad years will be lessened, though it can never, of course, be reduced to zero. Thus, in agricultural countries, the utilitarian should labour to improve facility of communication and irrigation.

In manufacturing countries he should, if he can find the means of doing so, aim for the same reason at diminishing the difference between years of abundant trade and years of depression. Much, perhaps, can be done in promoting this object by government, and little by private individuals. Government has every year a large amount of money to expend on ships and weapons, and public works, so that it can do much to encourage industry in bad years by large orders, and can discourage excessive production in good years, by refraining from giving custom to private firms. In this way government would, besides getting its work done cheaply, defend the nation against the pernicious effect of violent oscillations between periods of excessive prosperity and years of great depression.

So far, we have been considering the means of protection against famine and scarcity, to which vegetarian nations are especially exposed, but which also afflict, in a less degree, nations that indulge in a mixed diet. Let us now consider whether there are any means of alleviating the bad effects that the killing of animals must have upon butchers, and that the eating of animal food must have upon the butcher's customers by more or less diminishing their natural sympathy with pain and suffering. One obvious way to the attainment of this object is to introduce a more painless way of killing animals, than that at present practised. The killing of animals by the butcher is probably less painful than the natural death by disease that they would otherwise die. But, though such cruel practices as that called in French *saigner en blanc* are rare in England, death in the shambles is still much more painful to the animals killed, and much more horrifying to the tiro in the art of butchery, than it need be. Animals are too often kept for a long time huddled together without drink, in great heat, waiting their turn to die, and seeing, in the meantime, the death throes of their more fortunate companions. The natural remedy for this would be that animals should, before being slaughtered, be made to pass through a narcotic chamber as was proposed by Dr. Richardson, or that they should be killed by electricity. If this, however, should be rejected as too revolutionary a proposal, all that remains is to improve the shambles as far as is consistent with the continued employment of the knife and the pole-axe and the other lethal weapons now used. Also, a salve may be provided for the conscience of the butcher by teaching him that, in spite of all appearances to the

K

contrary, he does not really increase the sum of animal suffering. No doubt, many a butcher's mind is oppressed by the thought that his trade is a cruel one and repulsive to the best instincts of humanity. If in spite of such qualms of conscience he perseveres in a trade repulsive to his moral nature, then his moral nature must be impaired. He would be saved from much of this pain at the sight of the deaths of sheep and oxen and from the loss of happiness due to moral deterioration, if he could be taught the real facts of the case, namely that butchers substitute a less painful for a more painful death. For if all butchers gave up their profession in disgust, one of two results would follow. Either animals would be killed more painfully by unskilled amateur butchers, or vegetarianism would be adopted universally, and far more animals would die lingering deaths by disease and starvation. Therefore the butcher, if he considers the matter, has a perfect right to regard himself much in the same light as other men regard themselves, when they perform the unpleasant task of killing a painfully wounded animal outright, in order to put it out of misery.

Vegetarians not only advocate their system as likely to free the human world from want and starvation and the brute world from much pain which, as we have seen, are untenable claims, but also as improving the health of mind and body. Vegetarianism, they say, gives its followers " clearer intellects, purer blood, stronger muscles, healthier bodies." If it does so, utilitarians should adopt it. Clearer intellects are at least not obviously opposed to happiness, and health of body is productive of happiness. But whether vegetarianism is or is not conducive to health and strength is an open question. It was once generally supposed in England that plenty of beef and beer was absolutely necessary for great strength and good health. This false idea has been entirely exploded by the many instances of strong

and healthy vegetarian individuals and nations that
have been brought forward by the supporters of vegetarianism. But, on the other side, just as many good
instances of strong and healthy carnivorous nations and
individuals can be brought forward. Even if it could
be proved that vegetarianism improves the health and
strength of each individual who adopts it, there would
still remain the further question whether the individual
advantage, in the long run, promoted the general health.
But as vegetarians have not yet proved conclusively
even that every eater of flesh would be stronger and
healthier if he confined himself to vegetables, the
utilitarian will certainly not feel himself bound to
promote vegetarianism on the score of the improvement
of health.

There are two other arguments remaining in favour
of vegetarianism which are worthy of consideration.
The first is that butchers' shops are ugly sights even at
Christmas time when the carcasses are gaily decorated
with sprigs of holly, and arranged in the most elegant
combinations that the butcher's taste can devise. A
thing of ugliness is a pain for ever, but the amount
of pain that the contemplation of a butcher's shop
inflicts on the average individual of a nation, the
majority of which are meat eaters, is very small, and
even this moderate pain might be evaded without
introducing vegetarianism, if butchers were forbidden
to flaunt their repulsive wares in the front of their
shops.

The last argument to be mentioned in favour of
vegetarianism is of much greater importance. It is
found that vegetarians have very little inclination for
strong drinks. Almost always when a man becomes a
vegetarian, he desists from drinking beer, wine and
spirits. Thus vegetarianism is a very powerful instrument in favour of temperance and total abstinence.
If then it can be shown that total abstinence would

benefit the human race, the utilitarian should become an advocate of vegetarianism.

The principal facts that may be regarded as established on the subject of temperance are as follows. The consumption of alcoholic liquors is practically unproductive consumption. According to Liebig "nine quarts of the best ale contain as much nourishment as would lie on the point of a table-knife," and it is really established that intoxicants cannot be regarded as foods. On this unproductive consumption an immense amount of wealth is expended. In the British Isles alone the annual expenditure on intoxicating liquors amounts to about £136,000,000. If this were spent instead upon bread and other necessaries of life, the British Isles might support 2,700,000 more men, women, and children, allowing each individual man, woman, or child £50 a year. So that, if all the inhabitants of the British Isles were to become total abstainers, it would, as far as population is concerned, have about the same effect as the addition to the United Kingdom of a new Scotland equal to the present Scotland, without Lanarkshire. There is a large consensus of medical opinion that wine and spirits and ale, even in moderation, are either utterly useless or distinctly pernicious to almost everybody without exception, whether in good or bad health, whether engaged in mental or bodily labour. The records of insurance offices and provident clubs show that total abstainers live far longer than those in the list of moderate drinkers. Even allowing for the fact that many may be inscribed as moderate drinkers who are really immoderate, or afterwards become so, these lists seem to prove that the total abstainer has a better chance of living a long and healthy life than the average man. Strong drink ruins not only the body but also minds and morals. According to Lord Shaftesbury, 60 out of every 100 who enter asylums are made lunatics by drink, and every newspaper teems with crimes committed by drunkards. All this shows that a total abstainer has far more chance than a drinker of being wealthy, healthy, and wise. The fact that those who drink often enjoy themselves over their cups will hardly be considered to be an argument on the other side, when it is remembered that any unnatural exhilaration due to alcohol is punished on the morrow by a corresponding access of depression.

Is it not therefore incumbent on every utilitarian to go through the land, preaching and practising total abstinence ? This would be the necessary conclusion from the facts given above, if it were true that whatever is good for the individual is good for the whole human race or for the nation to which he belongs. But this we have seen, when considering medical science, to be not always the case. Granting that the drinking of strong drink resembles in its effect a widespreading and fatal disease, it may, like other diseases, by killing off the weaker members of each generation, tend to benefit the health of the succeeding generation.

In spite of the £136,000,000 spent annually on drink, the death-rate of the United Kingdom is very low as compared with the death-rate of other countries and with its own death-rate at other times. The history of the effect of strong drink upon English health would appear to have been roughly as follows. Up to about the end of the seventeenth century the English for the most part confined their potations to ale. To this mild intoxicant they had become adapted by the operation of natural selection during many generations, in which those, who were too weak or otherwise unable to drink beer and be healthy, had died out. At the end of this period the drinking of spirits became suddenly habitual. Gin, brandy, and whisky contain about seven times as much alcohol as beer, and are therefore far more destructive. The natural result of the sudden introduction of such powerful intoxicants among a nation of beer drinkers resembled the effect produced by small-pox or measles among a savage nation that has never before been attacked by these diseases. The greater perniciousness of spirits may be seen portrayed with horrible reality by Hogarth in his picture of " Beer Street and Gin Lane." It is probable that about this time the death-rate of England became higher than it ever was before or has ever been since. But gradually the marvellous adaptability of the human race came into play. Those who were too weak in mind or body to stand strong drink were weeded out in successive generations. The present generation is for the most part composed of the descendants of ancestors who could take a certain amount of strong drink without much harm to themselves.

It may, perhaps, when we consider the deleterious effects of strong drink, be wondered why the operation of natural selection has not made us a nation of total abstainers. Other things being equal, a total abstainer is more likely to live long, and become wealthy, and leave descendants behind him than one who drinks alcoholic drinks. How is it then that the drinkers of alcohol have not been stamped out in the struggle for existence ? The reason seems to be that abstinence from alcohol is not the only thing that gives advantage in the struggle for existence, and that there are other advantages which, as it so happens, are generally found in union with liking for strong drink. As a rule those who have a great fund of animal spirits, health, muscular strength, and energy are fond of wine and spirits, and by the vigorous exercise of mind and body due to these possessions, are able to bear a certain amount of alcohol without material injury. For, that a certain amount of alcohol may be consumed without much harm is admitted even by some of those whose general evidence is most distinctly in favour of total abstinence. " A minority of persons," we read in Dr. Richardson's lectures on alcohol, " who habitually take alcohol escape with impunity from injury. Some of these escape because they only subject themselves to it on a scale so moderate that they can scarcely be said to be under its spell. If they take it regularly, they never exceed an ounce to an ounce and a half of the pure spirit in the day ; and, if they indulge in a little more than this, it is only at recreative seasons, after which they atone for what they have done by a temporary total abstinence. Others take more freely than the above, but escape because they are physiologically constituted in such manner that they can rapidly eliminate the fluid from their bodies. These, if they are moderately prudent, may even go so far as to indulge in alcohol and yet suffer no material harm. But they are a limited few, if the term may be applied to them, who are so privileged." Just as some races of animals escape beasts of prey by developing strength, and others by swiftness, and as some men avoid committing vicious acts by strength of virtuous will, and others by fleeing from the world and its temptations, so some escape the evils of alcohol by splendid health, activity, and powers of self-restraining moderation, while others obtain the same result by pledging themselves to total abstinence. If it be asked why exuberant health in union with total abstinence should not be the characteristics of those likely to conquer in the struggle for existence, the answer is that perhaps eventually this combination may be the ordinary type of humanity. But at present this combination is very rare. There appears to be some incompatibility between the extreme of health and strength, and aversion to wine and spirits, just as in the animal world excessive strength and swiftness are rarely combined, in spite of the advantage such a combination would have over strength without great swiftness, or swiftness without great strength in the struggle for existence.

Thus the destructive effects of alcohol weed out excessive drinkers whether strong or weak, and also moderate drinkers who are only blessed with moderate health, strength, and power of eliminating the alcohol they consume. There are then left to be ancestors of coming generations for the most part those on the one hand whose great strength and activity enable them to take without material harm a limited amount of alcohol, and whose strength of will prevents their love of wine from leading them to excess, and on the other hand in small but perhaps gradually increasing numbers those who for their own sakes or as an example to their fellowmen, and because their delight in wine, ale, and spirits is not very great, become total abstainers. The utilitarian therefore in considering the temperance question will have to make up his mind which of these two classes of survivals is likely to be the happier on the average. Those who effectually preach total abstinence help to produce a world of total abstainers. Would such a world be happier than the descendants of exceptionally healthy moderate drinkers ?

With regard to health, it is not clear whether the world of total abstainers would have the advantage or not. It must be admitted that some of the descendants of moderate drinkers would be likely in each generation to degenerate into that excess in the use of alcohol which leads to delirium tremens, liver disease, consumption, kidney disease, paralysis, and insanity. Thus universal abstinence would diminish greatly the number of fatal diseases to which human beings are liable. In this way its effect on the average health of the human race would be much the same as some great medical discovery, as quinine, or vaccination, if in spite of the " Encyclopædia

Britannica" the worth of vaccination may be regarded as an established fact. However beneficial total abstinence may be to the individual, it does not follow that it is advantageous to the race. An ancient Briton would probably have added to his chance of health and long life by taking to wear clothes instead of painting himself blue with woad, but it does not follow that a clothes-wearing world would on the average be healthier or longer lived than a naked world. A civilised Greek once wondered how a half naked savage could endure a biting wind. The savage replied by asking him whether the cold wind hurt his face, and being answered in the negative said, " I am all face." Unclothed savages must die unless their bodies are as impervious to cold as the face of a man in clothes must be, and consequently all their skin becomes equally cold proof. In like manner, where alcohol is drunk, nations by the extinction of the unfit get strong enough to offer resistance to the deleterious effects of strong drink. Savages who have not been trained and weeded for generations by the fiery trial of alcohol, are in danger of being annihilated when strong European drinks are introduced into their midst. But if for a few generations they can survive, they may escape eventual extinction. This appears to have happened long ago in the case of the American negroes and later in the case of the American Indians. At first the latter were decimated by firewater and everyone thought that they would disappear off the face of the earth, seeing how rapidly they decreased in numbers. But now they have, as it were, turned the corner and are once more increasing. " By a careful study of the census," remarks the " Encyclopædia Americana " (1886), " it is noticed that most of the tribes are to-day on the increase." The remnant which is now left is doubtless the offspring of the few Red Indians who by self-control or physiological constitution could resist alcohol,

† Is this because they have become habituated to alcohol or because wars have ceased and they are better housed and fed?

In a few more generations it may be expected that the Red Indians may drink intoxicating liquors and be as healthy as they used to be in the old days of their enforced abstinence. If a nation can thus pass from abstinence to non-abstinence without eventually suffering in average health, it is likely that the world might pass from wine-drinking to abstinence without gaining in health by the change, the reason being that total abstinence would enable many weak persons, who would have died childless had they indulged in strong drink, to live and leave weak descendants behind them. This bad effect may just about counterbalance the good effect produced on the general happiness by the improvement in the health of those who, but for alcohol, would be absolutely healthy, or healthy above the average. Thus total abstinence does not seem to increase the happiness of the world by improving the average health.

But though total abstinence does not improve the health of the world, it may promote its happiness in other ways. At any rate, there is little fear of its diminishing the health of the world. So that, if in other respects it promotes happiness, the world would still be the gainer. Let us then, leaving the effect upon the general health an open question, consider how far temperance militates against and how far it promotes happiness. In the first place, there is no doubt that the human race derives a large amount of happiness from drinking wine. It is on account of this happiness that wine has been the subject of poetic praise from the earliest dawn of poetry to the present day. "Wine that maketh glad the heart of man" is ranked by the Psalmist with oil and bread, as one of the greatest of the gifts of God. In the last chapter of Proverbs it is recommended as the best medicine for the miserable. "Give strong drink," we read, "unto him that is ready to perish, and wine unto these that be of heavy hearts. Let him drink and

forget his poverty and remember his misery no more."[1]
Homer, speaking through the mouth of the wise Ulysses,
describes a feast accompanied by song and wine as the
acme of happiness. "I cannot say that aught is more
pleasing," remarks Ulysses to Alcinous, "than when
joy pervades a whole people, and the feasters, seated in
their places through the halls, listen to a bard, and the
tables are loaded with bread and flesh, and the cup-
bearer drawing wine from the bowl carries it round
and pours it into the cups." Many such strong evidences
in favour of the pleasures of wine might be culled from
the writings of sober serious writers without drawing
upon the lyrics of distinctly Bacchanalian poets like
Anacreon, Lovelace, and Burns. But it is unnecessary
to do so. Every one knows that poetry is full of the
praise of wine, and no one in his senses will venture to
maintain that all the chorus of praise is due to delusion.
What will be said is that all this mass of pleasure is
necessarily followed by a corresponding amount of pain,
that to the happiness of the convivial night the pain of
headache and depression of spirits on the morrow is
exactly proportionate. But the impartial consultation
of experience on the subject will show that this is not
really the case. There seems to be an idea in the minds
of many supporters of temperance when speaking of the
effects of wine, that each man has a definite amount of
potential energy and joy at his disposal, so that if by
means of the stimulation of wine you expend more
energy and feel more joy to-day, you thereby lessen

[1] " Gie him strong drink, until he wink,
    That's sinking in despair ;
  An' liquor guid to fire his bluid
    That's prest wi' grief and care ;
  There let him bouse and deep carouse,
    Wi' bumpers flowing o'er,
  Till he forgets his loves or debts,
    An' minds his griefs no more."—*Burns.*
Compare Horace Epistles 1, v. 16-20.

+ Poor Burns! He deserves a
letter setting forth than that!

your capabilities of energy and joy in the morrow. It is needless to say that this idea receives no support from the doctrine of the conservation of energy which teaches that there is a definite amount of energy in the universe, not that there is a definite unalterable amount of energy in each man, far less that there is a definite amount of capability of joy in each man. On the contrary, the man that is joyful to-day is often thereby fortified against misery on the morrow, just as a man who has been in a warm room is better able to bear the cold out of doors than one who has long been shivering in a cold place. The subsequent depression is proportionate rather to the amount of excess of wine drinking than to the joy felt at the time of drinking. It is certain that terrible depression often follows heavy drinking in which the drinker has had little or no pleasure, and it is quite possible that joy from very moderate drinking may be had without any subsequent depression. Weariness in the morning is proportionate to the amount of excessive exercise taken the day before, but moderate exercise is followed by no weariness after an ordinary good night's rest has intervened. Nevertheless, the excess that leads to depression is so common among drinkers, and is so much greater among hard drinkers than the pleasure they enjoy from their hard drinking, that, on the whole, it is probable that a drinking world suffers as much pain in the form of subsequent headache and depression as the pleasure it derives from drinking. An individual, who likes wine and knows that he can keep within the bounds of the strictest moderation, may gain the joy without the accompanying pain, and, as far as immediate effects are concerned, may enjoy life more with the help of wine than he could without it. But the same can hardly be said at present of any nation or of the whole human race. The utilitarian, therefore, finding it impossible to decide whether on the whole the pleasure of drinking is greater or less than the quickly following pain due to excess, will not, unless he takes other more remote effects into consideration, be able to decide whether he ought to exert himself in support of the cause of total abstinence or not.

One of these more remote effects, and a very important one, has been already indicated. Consumption of alcohol being unproductive decreases the population of the world, a result which should certainly be desired by the pessimistic utilitarian and opposed in every way by the optimistic utilitarian. Until, however, optimists have given us good reason to believe that the average man is happy, or pessimists have given good reason to believe that he is miserable, most utilitarians will disregard increase and decrease of population and only consider how average happiness may be promoted.

Total abstinence resembles vegetarianism in one of its felicific effects, in so far as it deprives nations who practise it of a convenient means of economy in years of scarcity. When famine is imminent, a people in the habit of spending much on alcoholic drinks can easily avoid starvation by curtailing its expenditure on the luxury of drink. Thus the practice of drinking strong drink, like that of eating animal food, is useful as a kind of insurance against famine, and so tends to promote happiness.

We saw above that the good effects of eating animal food as a preventive of famine were about counterbalanced by its evil effects on the minds of butchers in particular and of the general meat-eating public. Similar bad effects are also found to follow from the drinking of strong drink. Here, too, we find one particular class of the population exposed to influences of a peculiarly brutalising character. The publican must shut his heart against the cruel effect of his liquor upon his customer, just as the butcher must render himself insensible to sympathy with animal pain; and, inasmuch as drunkards suffer far more pain than slaughtered animals, his moral nature must be more impaired by the necessity of so doing. Also the particular class thus injuriously affected is much greater. Whereas there were in 1881 about 84,000 butchers and poulterers in England and Wales, the number of innkeepers and their servants at the same time amounted to 132,000, and there were 70,000 brewers, wine-merchants, and others engaged in the sale and manufacture of strong drink to supply public and private houses. But it is when we come to consider the general public, that we see the evil effects of strong drink on the moral character to be far worse than the evil effects of meat-eating. The worst that can be said of meat-eaters is that if they reflect, they may think, and that wrongly, their mode of life to be prejudicial to animal happiness. Vegetarians often urge that the eating of animal food produces a certain amount of ferocity in man like that which distinguishes the carnivorous animals, but this is a very doubtful assertion. The tremendous demoralising effect of drinking is capable of overwhelming demonstration, and may be confirmed in the police reports of every newspaper we happen to open. If any one likes to read in a consecutive form some typical examples of the horrible crimes to which drunkenness leads, let him get a book called "Legion, or the Modern Demoniac" by W. Gilbert. The book is not pleasant reading, but it is useful as giving a collection of facts throwing a lurid light on the effects of strong drink. The Lord Chief Justice perhaps scarcely exaggerated the amount of crime due to drink when he gave it as his opinion that "but for drink we might shut up nine out of ten of our gaols." And it must be remembered that, besides the overt convicted crime due to drink, there must be an infinite number of vicious acts due to the same cause that escape the clutches of the law. The amount of misery due to all these offences against

law and morality committed under the influence of
drink is incalculable, and the whole burden would be
shaken off, if total abstinence became the universal rule.
With the prospect of such a diminution of crime before
our eyes, we can say little in favour of ale, wine, and
spirits. The transitory joy of moderate drinking is
cancelled by the heavy depression of the large proportion of drinkers who are sure to drink too much.
As far as can be seen, owing to the regulative action
of natural selection, drinking does not injuriously affect
average health, nor yet does it improve health. There
only remains the good effect of alcoholic drinks, which
it shares with all other wasteful expenditure, as a means
of insurance against famine, but this advantage as
compared with the immense reduction of crime that
would be brought about by total abstinence, must
promptly kick the beam. Therefore the utilitarian is
bound by his principles to promote the cause of total
abstinence by all possible means, and especially by
becoming himself a total abstainer, as that is the most
effective way of promoting the cause.

As the utilitarian by promoting abstinence, while defending the people against temptation to crime, exposes
them to famine, he should try his best to provide by
other means against danger of famine. The danger of
famine due to vegetarianism and total abstinence, fortunately tends to work its own cure, because, wherever
real danger is manifest, precautionary measures are
more easily adopted. It will be more easy to demon-
strate the necessity of insurance against scarcity to a
people consisting of vegetarians and total abstainers,
because they really are in more danger than meat eaters
and wine drinkers. They will have, in their greater
and well warranted fear, a stronger stimulus to secure
regularity in the annual produce of wealth, and, since
such regularity will always be more or less unattainable, to lay by in good years, as much as can be spared

+ Without liquor, in our Occidental countries we should be practically insured against scarcity.

to keep them from starvation in the bad years. We
have seen that irrigation tends to produce more regularity in the amount of agricultural production, and
that facility of communication alleviates the distress of
bad years. What remains to be done is to encourage
the practice of insurance in its more readily recognised
forms. Either the nation as a whole, or individuals,
must be taught to provide funds of savings for their
support in times of scarcity. The same object may be
obtained by raising the standard of comfort, and teaching the average man to regard a certain amount of
luxury as essential to his existence. Only he must learn
to set his heart on less pernicious luxuries than alcoholic drink, and even than tobacco, which, comparatively
harmless in itself, often leads to the consumption of
strong drinks. When, by prudence and late marriage,
the population is somewhat diminished, and it is found
possible to secure the requisites of a higher standard of
comfort, it must not be supposed that those living up
to the new standard, are any happier than their fathers
who lived up to a lower standard. The new idea of
comfort will have produced desires commensurate with
the improved comfort obtained, and the new luxuries,
having become the common possession of the average
man, will cease to afford exceptional satisfaction. But
each individual, and therefore the whole people, will
suffer less from bad years, as the average man will then
merely revert to bare necessaries, instead of to extreme
want and starvation.

Vegetarians and total abstainers may also be defended
against the effect of misfortune by life assurance—an
arrangement by which wives and children are defended against destitution, in the case of the early
death of a husband and father, and by which people
generally can protect themselves and their families, to
a certain extent, against heavy loss from illness and
accidents. It may be described in sporting phrase as a

kind of hedging against extreme misfortune by an agreement between a certain number of persons, namely, those who take policies in the same office, that those who are fortunate shall give support to those who are unfortunate. Thus insurance tends to equalise the lot of all insurers. Those, who die young, or incur the particular misfortunes insured against, gain by insurance, while those who live long, and do not suffer from the illness or accidents, or other misfortune, against which they insured themselves, are pecuniarily losers; for, if they had invested their money in other investments, they would probably have been richer. This system has, without doubt, when applied in its natural and most common way, considerably alleviated the misery of mankind. We have before seen reason to believe, that the same amount of means to happiness produces more happiness when equally, than when unequally distributed, because the loss of ten pounds' worth of the necessaries of life causes more pain to a poor man, than the addition of ten pounds' worth of luxury gives to a rich man. The difference between the misery of uninsured orphans, widows, and men incapacitated for work, or attacked by sudden misfortune, and the less misery which they would suffer if protected by insurance, is greater than the loss of happiness owing to waste of wealth incurred by those who have insured against misfortune, and been long-lived and fortunate. Further, there must be taken into account the peace of mind of the man who has been prudent enough to insure himself against misfortune, as compared with the anxiety about the future in the heart of the man who has not insured himself, and those dearest to him, against sudden and overwhelming calamity. Thus, there are two great advantages secured by insurance. On the other side, it may be said, that insured persons will be less careful to avoid danger. This is true, but only to a very limited extent, and, in

L

some occupations, it is a duty to face danger boldly, so that, in some cases, insurance helps men to do their duty well. A more grave objection is the misuse of insurance, in the heavy insurance of unseaworthy ships, and young children. But these abuses can be checked by legislative interference. It is not difficult to answer a plausible argument against life assurance based on the fact that it encourages marriages and so tends to increase the over-population of the world. There is, indeed, no doubt that young men, who would otherwise have remained single, are enabled to marry by the possibility of insuring their lives and so defending their families against destitution in the event of their early death. But this is no evil, but rather a defence against a great danger. The reckless marriages of the improvident have long threatened to drive prudence out of the world by causing a large portion of each new generation to be children inheriting improvidence from improvident parents. Whatever encourages the prudent to marry must surely have a beneficial effect on the future of the human race. So, after considering possible objections, we may come to the conclusion, that the institution of insurance has promoted the happiness of the world, and that the practice should be encouraged by utilitarians, especially among nations of vegetarians and total abstainers.

CHAPTER X.

To the question whether virtue promotes the general happiness, the utilitarian replies that virtuous action means action productive of happiness, and that therefore it would be a contradiction in terms to say that any particular virtuous action diminished happiness. He may, however, reasonably discuss what classes of virtuous action are most productive of happiness, and it will be his duty to point out for the benefit of his fellowmen that certain actions which they consider virtuous are not really so, because they do not promote or because they actually diminish the sum of happiness.

The latter task will involve him in some difficulties. Supposing another person who is not a utilitarian does an act, thinking it to be virtuous, although it diminishes happiness, must utilitarians regard it as vicious ? If they do so, then they disapprove of the action of a man who acted in accordance with the dictates of his conscience, and consider that he would have been less blameworthy, had he acted in opposition to the dictates of his conscience. This seems to be such a paradoxical ethical conclusion that it can hardly be accepted. Surely even utilitarians must admit that the man who obeys his conscience is better than the man who disobeys its commands. Possibly, in such a case, they would distinguish between the act and the agent, and consider that it was a bad act, *i.e.*, an act productive of misery, although the agent showed his goodness by doing it because he thereby manifested a characteristic, namely the tendency to obey conscience, which would in ninety-nine cases out of a hundred, produce good acts, acts productive of happiness. Or they may consider the act under consideration to be, on account of the agent's state of mind, more felicific and therefore better than another possible action, which, had it not been condemned by his unenlightened conscience, would have been more felicific, admitting that those who are not utilitarians must not be judged by the same standards as utilitarians, just as modern moralists do not think it right to judge the ancients by the modern moral standard which they apply to their own actions. They might thus know the act to be the best act open to the other man who is not a utilitarian, although they themselves, being utilitarians, could not do it without immorality. And this is perhaps the better solution of the difficulty, which is not, however, of very great importance. For, ethics being practical, a standard is valuable not for settling theoretic questions, but rather as a means to right action, and for this purpose it is only necessary that we should be able to judge our own conduct, not that we should judge that of others. The difficulty considered above does not come in the way of a utilitarian in judging his own conduct, for, if his conscience approved of an action which he knew would diminish happiness, he would not be a utilitarian.

But how, it may be asked, can he praise or blame aright, if he has no standard to apply to the actions of others ? The answer is that the outward expression of praise or blame is an act of his own, which, like his other acts, must be determined by the application of his moral standard. He must praise an act if he thinks that his praise of it will promote the happiness of the world, and blame it if he thinks his blame of it will diminish the happiness of the world, whatever may be his inward feelings of approval or disapproval. Thus it may be incumbent on the utilitarian to praise an action that he would not do himself, and blame an action that his morality would urge him to do if he were in the same position as the actor. For instance, let us consider the promise of James Douglas to take the Bruce's heart to Palestine. A utilitarian, consulted before the promise was given, might have said to Douglas, " Do not promise, for by your departure, and probable death, you will denude Scotland of her best defenders and expose her to invasion and anarchy." But, after Douglas is dead, and neither praise nor blame can undo the evil done in this particular case, he will look rather to the general effects of his words, and will praise Douglas's devotion to his friend, knowing that such devotion only in very exceptional cases diminishes happiness, and that therefore it ought to be encouraged. But the utilitarian who, after Douglas's death, praises his deed, would not perhaps have felt justified in doing it himself. He would probably think that the general good effect of the example given in this brilliant act of devotion is less than the diminution of happiness incurred by Scotland, and therefore by the world, as there is no reason to believe that the happiness that Douglas's presence would have secured to Scotland would have been at the expense of any other part of the world. Similarly a utilitarian might consistently, after the event, express disapproval of Harold for breaking his promise to William, even though he may suppose that the Saxon prince had every reason to believe that the violation of his oath was likely to benefit England and the human race. If he does express disapproval, it will be on the ground of the necessity of discouraging, by words as well as acts, the generally infelicific practice of oath-breaking. In all such cases, however, the utilitarian will have carefully to take into consideration the evil that may accrue from his con-cealment of his true sentiments.

For the bad effects of falsehood are so great that

it is doubtful whether the utilitarian is ever justified in being untruthful in the least degree. The evils produced by untruthfulness are the lessening of mutual confidence, the bad example given to others, and the degradation of the soul of the deceiver. Imaginary circumstances may be conceived in which these effects are so slight that they would scarcely be taken into account, while the pain that will follow the truth is great and undoubted. For instance, let A, a utilitarian, know a secret, the knowledge of which would embitter the rest of B's life, and which he can only conceal from B by a lie. Further, let there be no chance of A's lie being ever discovered. Each of these conditions is in itself quite possible, though they may not, perhaps, ever all three be combined in fact. But if they were, since according to the hypothesis the lie could never be detected, there would be no impairment of confidence and no bad example. Nor would the liar's soul be degraded, as, being a utilitarian, he would think he had done a virtuous action. But it so seldom happens that one has a chance of telling a lie with the certainty of its never being discovered, that the utilitarian ought, perhaps, to act through life on the simpler rule of unswerving truthfulness even when he is speaking to sick persons, brigands, children, or idiots. The mutual confidence engendered by such strict truthfulness would, it may be argued, do so much to promote happiness as to more than compensate for the death of a few sick persons who might otherwise have recovered, and the saving of one or two lives from brigands, especially as such saving of life can only be effected in a limited number of instances. For sick persons, knowing that lies are told them, refuse to believe and are irritated often in a way to make them more ill by the knowledge that they are being deceived by those around them, and brigands must often be induced to kill, or subject to cruel confinement, their victims, by the fact that they cannot believe their victims' promises and so cannot without great difficulty arrange for a ransom. Therefore, absolute truthfulness would, perhaps, be the best rule for the utilitarian to adopt. At any rate he should preach no other to the world, for the majority of mankind being unable properly to estimate the importance of impairment of confidence, as compared with the effect upon some particular person or persons whom a lie seems likely to benefit, are sure, if they allow themselves occasional deviations from truth, to use that liberty far more than utilitarian considerations really allow.

But it is an old and good moral rule that a man must practise what he preaches. Can this rule be violated without bad effects by a utilitarian, if he can keep secret the discrepancy between his preaching and his practice? This secrecy may deprive the discrepancy of its usual bad effects upon others, namely, the encouragement of untruthfulness by example, and the contempt in which they are induced to hold moral maxims by seeing them transgressed by those who profess them. But in spite of secrecy the bad effect on the utilitarian himself will hardly fail to remain. He can scarcely make a resolution of consistent hypocrisy to extend through his whole life without injuriously affecting his own character. For he will, perhaps, by habit become reconciled to deceit and extend the practice to cases in which it is not really excusable on utilitarian grounds, and the feeling that, if the truth were known, he would be despised by his fellowmen will degrade him in his own eyes and diminish his self-respect. This feeling of degradation will much diminish his own happiness, which is a part of the general happiness as important as anybody else's happiness. These considerations, most of which apply not merely to the teaching of moral doctrine that the teacher does not think binding on himself, but also to lies told with the intention of promoting happiness, are so strong that the utilitarian will have good reason to doubt whether it would not be better to bind himself once for all to unswerving obedience to truth in all its forms, not merely to verbal truth. Of course it is impossible for any man entirely to prevent others from forming misconceptions about his character and principles of action, but the utilitarian standard would at any rate seem to require us not to act in such a way as would be certain to cause widespread misconception and make men form a higher opinion of us than they would have, if they knew our true principles. Therefore the utilitarian must not preach conduct that he would not practise.

Justice will mean to the utilitarian distribution of rewards and punishments and other objects of desire and aversion in such a way as may be best for the general happiness. This will generally consist in equal distribution when there is no reason for inequality, in satisfaction of ordinary expectations, and in reward or punishment according to desert, if there is such a thing as free will or desert. But all kinds of distribution are, in the eyes of the utilitarian, desirable or undesirable, not in themselves, but as means to the promotion of happiness. Thus the utilitarian may approve of and call just the institution of private property, because it encourages labour, and labour promotes happiness, or because it exists and its abolition would cause unhappiness, or he may condemn it as prejudicial to happiness and therefore unjust. How far can a utilitarian go in the way of neglect of reward according to desert and in inequality of distribution in order to promote the interests of happiness? The answer is that he must go to any length. Otherwise he is not a pure utilitarian. For, if he attaches any importance to equality or reward of desert when opposed to the promotion of happiness, instead of having one

moral first principle, he has two or three, which may
perhaps come into conflict. For instance, the very
unequal distribution of the good things of life due to
the institution of private property, if justice is not
determined entirely by the utilitarian standard, might be
supposed by the same man to be unjust, because it
does not reward men according to their virtue, and yet
productive of happiness. It is conceivable that
happiness might be promoted by distributions far
more unequal and far more opposed to the principle
of reward according to desert than the distribution
of property. Let us take an extreme case. Suppose
that a utilitarian, who knows himself to be not very
virtuous, were convinced that by depriving every one
of a hundred men more virtuous and already more
miserable than himself, of one degree of happiness, he
could add 101 degrees to his own happiness without
diminishing the happiness of the rest of the world,
as a utilitarian, he would be bound to make this
astounding sacrifice of others to self, if he wished
to act strictly in accordance with the principles of
his morality. Generally utilitarianism leads to altruistic
conduct, because utilitarians generally agree with
Paley and Mill, that the promotion of the happiness of
others is always the best means of promoting one's
own happiness. So closely connected, indeed, are
altruism and utilitarianism, owing to the usual
acceptance by utilitarians of this assumption, that
they are often confounded together as equivalent
terms, meaning the opposite of egoism. Nevertheless
it is easy to see that the man in the hypothetical
case we are considering, who, in accordance with his
principles, sacrifices the less happiness of many others
to his own greater happiness, promotes the aggregate
happiness of the world and therefore is really a utilitarian, although his conduct is free from all tincture of
altruism. Therefore, anyone who cannot believe in a

morality that might in certain conceivable circumstances bid him be happy at the expense of large numbers of his fellowmen, ought to give up all claim to be a utilitarian.

Utilitarians, who accept this conclusion and admit that utilitarianism in conceivable cases might be opposed to altruism, may perhaps try to make out that the conclusion under consideration only appears paradoxical owing to the common confusion between happiness and objects which are generally productive of happiness. No doubt, there is a danger of such a misunderstanding. Many persons when asked to consider the case of 101 degrees of happiness obtained by subtracting 100 degrees of happiness from 100 fellowmen, would, owing to the difficulty of measuring happiness, translate the instance into numerable material objects, and think perhaps of a man who, for £100 abstracted from 100 men, is enabled to buy as many objects of desire as they could have obtained for £101. This might be the case if a man, living in England, abstracted money from men living in Australia, where objects of desire are dearer. In such a case, if we look beyond the money and the objects of desire that may be purchased for the money, there is almost sure to be a great waste of happiness. The pain of losing a pound is usually greater than the pleasure of gaining one. In this case, the pains of loss would probably be intensified by a sense of injustice, and the pleasures of gain would be diminished by consciousness of meanness. Then there would be the after effects of the action to be considered. The gainer would have done an act that would be a step in the formation of the habit of robbing others for himself, which habit would be sure to cause unhappiness to himself and others. The losers would be inclined to retaliate on him, or, if they could not do that, they would be tempted to do to others as had been done to them. All these evils, though difficult to express in numerical form, would far out-balance the one pound worth of advantage which at first sight seemed to be added to the world by the transfer of property, so much so, that we should, perhaps, if we must express in pounds, shillings, and pence, an example of the transfer of happiness from many to one, so that the sum of happiness may really be increased, think of a man, who, by depriving 100 men of an aggregate sum of one hundred pence, gets as many objects of desire as they could purchase for £100. And even this might not perhaps satisfy the requirements of the case, for it is possible and not improbable, that one man deprived without compensation of a penny or a farthing, might from the sense of wrong suffer more pain than could be cancelled by the whole pleasure, that the spoiler gains by the possession or expenditure of £1000. So hard it is to estimate pleasure by money or any other standard. At any rate, the defender of utilitarianism will be able to show that transfers of sources of happiness, without compensation to the losers and against the will of the losers, can only promote the happiness of the world when the gainer gains very much more happiness from the source of happiness transferred, than the loser loses. When the gain is very much greater than the loss, even those who ordinarily admire altruism would not condemn the man who sacrificed others to himself. For instance, it would not appear paradoxical to approve of a starving man who stole a biscuit, that he could not get by any other means, nor would he be more condemned, if, to assimilate our instance to the hypothetical case we first put forward, we suppose the bakery, from which he steals the biscuit, to be a co-operate concern, consisting of 100 shareholders. Of course, in such a case, there would be other bad effects besides the loss of the shareholders in the bakery, but, perhaps, the aggregate

bad effects would be less than the pleasure or diminution of pain secured by the thief. From a consideration of such instances, the utilitarian might argue,
that, after all, there is nothing so very paradoxical
in maintaining that, in cases where the happiness of
the world is really promoted by a man's depriving others
of happiness and taking it to himself, he ought to do so.

Yet, after all, after giving due allowance for the fact
that as a rule a man cannot make himself happy at
the expense of others, except in cases where he transfers to himself something that promotes his happiness
a hundred times more than it could promote the happiness of those from whom he takes it, there remain
certain exceptional cases in which the utilitarian will
add to the happiness of the world by sacrificing
others to himself in a way that no ordinary moralist
would approve. Let there be two men in the position
of Pylades and Orestes. One is to die and the other
is to live, and they may settle by mutual agreement
which is to survive. Let Pylades be a melancholy
man who takes little pleasure in life, and having
no great desire to live is willing to consent to die.
Let Orestes be a jovial, happy-tempered man, who
thoroughly enjoys life. Would not Orestes, if a utilitarian, say to himself, "I derive much more pleasure
from life than Pylades. The world will have as good
an example of self-sacrifice given in the death of
Pylades for me, as it would have, were I to die for
him. My conscience not being delicate will not reproach me, indeed, as it is a utilitarian concience, it
will rather approve of me for acting in such a way
as seems likely to promote the world's happiness.
Therefore I am morally bound to let Pylades die."
Yet no ordinary moralist would allow that Orestes
in such a case showed virtue by living, and would be
less virtuous if he died. Ordinary morality approves
a victory of altruism over egoism, even where victory

decreases the happiness of the world. But what would a utilitarian do, if he were in the place of Orestes under the hypothetical circumstances given above? Altruism is carried to such lengths by the best utilitarians, that under such circumstances they would probably choose what ordinary moralists would call the better part, and make utilitarian yield to altruistic considerations. But if they did so, and defended such conduct as morally justifiable, they would so far cease to be utilitarians.

In reward and punishment the utilitarian will not always think it right to requite according to desert. For he cannot, without infringing his utilitarianism, acknowledge the absolute necessity of requiting good desert and bad desert. The acknowledgment of good and bad desert involves the acceptance of a new moral principle, " Men ought to be requited according to their desert," which might conflict with the utilitarian first principle, " We ought to act in such a way as to promote the greatest amount of happiness." For in certain cases happiness may best be promoted by forbearing to punish the guilty and reward the meritorious. As a rule, when a man has done a wicked deed, it is expedient in the interests of happiness to punish him, in order that the punishment may deter him from repeating his crime and others from imitating it. But as punishment is painful, if the same good results can be obtained by any other means, the utilitarian will prefer those other means. If, for instance, it could be arranged that criminals should be taken to some delightful region where they could enjoy themselves for the rest of their life, and all the while it was generally believed that they were being severely punished for their crimes, the utilitarian would prefer this to the ordinary method of punishment by painful imprisonment and death. As it happens, such arrangements are practically impossible, at any rate on a large scale. In individual cases, however, something like it may be done. Suppose a criminal has done a crime which is only known to me and which can be concealed from the rest of the world, and that, as may well be the case, there is more chance of reforming him by kindness than by inflicting painful punishment, then on utilitarian principles I should be bound not to punish him according to his desert. Also in some cases it is not productive of happiness to reward an act of good desert. Virtuous men that do good for its own sake promote the happiness of the world more than men who do good in the hope of reward. Therefore the utilitarian should indeed reward ordinary average men for their meritorious actions, but, when he meets with men who are capable of rising to the higher unselfish virtue, he should shrink from rewarding them for fear of encouraging them always to look for reward for their good actions.

Thus the utilitarian can only accept the duty of requiting according to desert as an inferior moral rule which must always yield when it conflicts with the utilitarian principle. It can only come into force, if at all, when the utilitarian is deliberating between courses of action and has no reason to believe that the one will promote happiness more than the other. In such a case, utilitarian considerations affording no guidance, he may guide himself by considerations of desert.

So far we have been assuming our utilitarian to be a believer in Free Will and difference of desert among human beings. But very many utilitarians are determinists, and therefore cannot believe that good men really deserve better treatment than bad men. For if bad men do their bad acts necessarily as a result of the previous history of the world, they cannot deserve punishment any more than a tempest or an avalanche, although it may be expedient from utilitarian considerations to punish them in order to provide them with a motive for avoiding the repetition of such acts. Good men cannot, if determinism is a fact, deserve reward more than good trees which bring forth good fruit, although it may be expedient to reward them just in the same way as it is expedient to prune and water the good fruit tree. If then the utilitarian is a determinist, he will believe that no man has any desert. He may still believe the proposition that men ought to be requited according to their desert when utilitarian considerations do not intervene, or when he thinks requital according to desert will promote general happiness. Therefore in such cases, since $o = o$, and men having all no desert have an equal amount of desert, he will try to reward all men equally by making them all equally happy. If a villain is, as is generally the case, more miserable than a philanthropist, he will, if utilitarian considerations are in favour of, or not opposed to, requital according to desert, take away from the philanthropist any source of happiness that he can confer on the villain, in order to equalise their lot as is required by the principle of reward according to desert.

Under Benevolence the utilitarian might include the whole of moral duty. He may be said to practise that virtue when he speaks the truth, keeps his promises, rewards virtue and punishes vice, gives just judgment, and abstains from excess. For in these, as in all his actions, he strives to do as much good as he can to his fellowmen. But perhaps he might give the term a rather less wide extent and call any action benevolent in which a man moved by affection or compassion promotes the happiness of the world by giving something of his own to his fellowmen whether it be money, or time, or trouble, or kindly words. The scope of the virtue would still be sufficiently large to include a good deal more than charity in the ordinary sense of the word.

Also a great deal of charity as ordinarily practised would be condemned by the utilitarian as not being true benevolence. For charity in an indiscriminate form has long been known to do more harm than good, at any

rate to the recipient. At first sight the most obvious
way to promote the happiness of the world would be to
keep just enough to feed and clothe oneself and give the
rest to the poor whom one sees begging from door to
door. But experience shows that such charity encourages begging and idleness. Wherever there are a
large number of persons who make a practice of giving
money just because they are asked, beggars are sure to
abound, and men who would otherwise have had to
work prefer the more precarious means of subsistence
opened to them. A large amount of money is still given
annually in this indiscriminate charity in spite of
the teaching of political economists, who show that, if
this money had not been given away to beggars, either
it would, unless hoarded, have been paid as wages for
work to labourers employed directly by the owners of the
money, or else it would have been invested as capital in
some industrial enterprise, and so have helped to pay the
labourers employed therein. Thus men who give away
money in this way simply in effect transfer money from men
who labour to men who beg. "No," it will be answered,
"they rather transfer money from those who can labour
and support themselves to those unfortunate beings
who can not do so." This is, however, not the case.
Many who beg are quite able to work but do not do
so, either because there is no work given them to do,
or because they think they can support themselves
by begging. It would be better and happier for them
to get money paid them for work whether done
willingly or unwillingly, as they might have, if the
greater portion of the money now given in indiscriminate charity were expended instead on labour. But
even if the lazy and unemployed men able to work
were taken away, some beggars would still remain
who are really unfit to support themselves by work.
Also there are some few poor men who are temporarily
or permanently unfit for work and yet too proud to

beg. These two classes of men and women are generally considered to be the most deserving recipients of charity, and the great object of organised charity is to distinguish them from those who can work but won't work.

Is then discriminate charity an effective instrument for promoting happiness? It does not discourage industry and thrift and reward idleness and imprudence, or, at least, it does not do so nearly as much as indiscriminate charity. For charity, whatever form it takes, must, to a certain extent, discourage the inclination to make careful and adequate provision for a rainy day. If a labourer through illness is unable to support himself and his family, he could not well be rejected as an unfit object of charity, and still less the widow and children of a poor worker who dies and leaves them destitute. Yet labourers sometimes save up money, so that, if they fall ill, they may not be dependent on charity; or they effect the same object by subscribing to a Trades' Union which will be bound to support them if they should be thrown out of work, and they can insure their lives in order that their death may not leave their families destitute. Some would make such provision, whether they had hopes of charitable relief or not; others would not do so, even if there were no hope of charity. Between these two extremes there must be an intermediate class who waver between the pleasure of spending all their wages and the duty of making provision for misfortune. To such the fair prospect of help in distress afforded by the practice of discriminate charity must incline the balance in favour of improvidence. And this is the case not only with the poor, but also with men who are rich and earn high salaries only as long as they are in good health. Among men in such a position there will always be found a certain number who are deterred from making by insurance an adequate or any provision for their family, because they feel confident that their friends and relations

M

would help their destitute families in case of their
decease.

But, it may be asked, is not relief by charitable
assistance, whether of friends or relations, or of
strangers, as productive of happiness as provision made
by thrift ?   At first sight it would seem to be in one
respect even more productive of happiness, as the giving
and receiving might naturally be supposed to excite
mutual kindliness.   It does so in some cases, but in
others, and perhaps in the majority of cases, the pre-
valent feelings are rather the painful ones of helpless
dependence on one side and grudging discontent at the
necessity of giving on the other.   The feeling of
grudging discontent is strongest when the recipient
of charity is strong and apparently able to work for
a subsistence, and ought to be, and is generally less,
when charity is given to the weak in mind or body,
who are also just the persons who would suffer most
from the entire discontinuance of charity.   Owing to
defects of mind and body which seem to be ineradicable
in the human race, there will always be some members
of society incapable of supporting themselves, and, even
among the most advanced utilitarians, charity will be pre-
valent.   Of course the incidence of the duty may be altered.
It may be decided that the weaker members of society
should be supported by their own families, rather than by
the community at large or philanthropists not connected
with them.   If this view is accepted, the philanthropist
will cease to bestow his charity upon strangers, on the
ground that a good prospect of being relieved from the
burden of supporting their needy relatives only makes
people less thrifty than they would otherwise be.   But
this would lead not to the extinction of charity but
to the substitution of one kind of charity for another.
What then must a utilitarian philanthropist do, who has
far more money to give away than is enough to support
the infirm members of his family ?   It is very doubtful

whether he can increase the happiness of the world more by giving away his abundant superfluity in charity, than by investing it with apparent selfishness in profitable business. All that we can say is that if he gives in charity to strangers, he should do so in such a way as least to discourage thrift, that is to say, he should relieve by it misery due to earthquakes, or floods, or such other catastrophes against which it is practically impossible for the sufferers to insure themselves. At the same time he should remember that, if he relieves the sufferings of Chinese or Japanese labourers by charity, he will, though helping on by his example the spread of universal world-wide sympathy, be less able to afford employment to English labourers. If our philanthropist resolves to invest his money, he may undoubtedly affect happiness by the manner of his investment. He would, for instance, decrease happiness by investing money in the slave trade, and would increase it by encouraging some industry, in which slave-hunters and the negroes they hunt could peaceably work together. This enquiry, however, cannot well be followed out to the end in this chapter, as, except when the investment considered is likely to bring pecuniary loss to the owner, it can scarcely come under the head of charity. The exhaustive investigation of the felicific or infelicific effects of various investments would indeed almost cover the whole field of the treatise. For money may be so used as to promote medical science, knowledge, art, social reforms, and all the other means of affecting happiness which we have discussed or have left undiscussed.

The strict limitation of charity prescribed above only applies to utilitarians, and only to those utilitarians, who see clearly the bad effects of indiscriminate charity, and the danger that always accompanies, more or less, the best regulated charity. Even in their case there is a danger that they may make themselves, by their reputation for niggardliness and selfishness, very un-

popular in the society to which they belong, and that
this unpopularity may decrease the happiness of the
world by making them unhappy themselves, and by
preventing them from using their influence effectually
in schemes to promote the happiness of others. To the
average man the utilitarian will only, with the greatest
caution, prescribe limitation of charity. For most men
are so strongly urged by their conscience to charity,
that they could not strictly restrain their charitable
impulses without doing violence to their moral nature.
Such violation of conscience is, of course, extremely
undesirable from the utilitarian point of view. The
utilitarian thinks it best of all that the whole world
should have a utilitarian conscience and obey it. But,
while this consummation devoutly to be wished is far
from attainment, he thinks it second best that men
should obey their own consciences, knowing, as he does,
that the conduct prescribed by ordinary morality is
almost always such as is likely to promote the world's
happiness. Thus, in the case of charity, the principal
hedonistic results to be considered are, (1) the surplus
remaining, after the happiness lost to those who would
have received the money in wages is subtracted from
the happiness conferred on those who receive the money
as a gift, (2) the good effects produced on the giver by
doing an act which will strengthen his habit of obeying
conscience, (3) the increase of sympathy due to the inter-
change of kindly acts, (4) the pleasant feeling of moral
approbation felt by the giver; and on the other side, (1)
the discouragement of thrift and industry, (2) the feeling
of dependence and inferiority on the part of the recipient,
(3) the grudge felt by the giver. It is not likely that
all these results will follow each act of charity. Some
indeed are scarcely compatible with each other. Alms
given grudgingly can hardly increase sympathy or afford
the giver a glow of moral approbation. In most or all
cases some of the results will be present and others absent,

and generally there will be considerable difficulty in deciding whether the good or bad effects predominate.

Charity is too often rather a redistribution than an increase of happiness. Other forms of benevolence are much more certain means of increasing happiness than the giving away of money and money's worth. The man who gives kindly words and wise counsel to his fellowmen is much surer of increasing happiness than he who gives them money, for such kindness can scarcely harm the recipients, and is not given at the expense of other men. Each man has only a certain amount of wealth at his disposal. If he gives away to one, he has the less left for others. But the saying of a kindly word of sympathy does not in the least diminish a man's power of uttering similar words of sympathy in the future to other men. The same is true in a less degree of actions of help which do not consist in the giving of money, such as saving a man from drowning, or even such small services as pointing out carefully the way to a wanderer. Every man in the course of his life neglects many such opportunities of aiding his fellowmen which will never return again. If a man regrets not having given money to a beggar, he still has the money he might have given, and can easily satisfy his conscience by giving it later on to another beggar. But, if I neglect an opportunity of preventing a railway accident, or detaching a tin-kettle from the tail of an unhappy dog, the opportunity is gone for ever. It is true that other opportunities of helping men or dogs will present themselves, but the neglect of the past opportunity does not in any way make it easier for me to use the later opportunities of rendering assistance that may present themselves.

Among these acts and words of kindness which add considerably to the happiness of the world, must be reckoned the courtesies of civilised society. Every act and word of politeness is intended to evince a desire to please, and, as a matter of fact, the polite man gives much more pleasure or less pain to the society in which he moves, than the rude man. It is objected that the rude man is often, at heart, a lover of his fellowmen, while the polite man may be a villain, and that a polite villain is likely in the long run to cause more unhappiness than a benevolent, but rude man. This is true. But it must be remembered that the rude man is just as likely to be a villain as the polite man, and that benevolence obscured by rudeness does less good than if it were recommended by polite manners. Another objection made against politeness is that it often makes us do for others, what they do not want or could do as well themselves. Why, for instance, it is said, should a weak man offer his arm to a strong lady who crosses a drawing-room or open the door for her ? Are not such mere pretences of rendering help absurd ? These acts of polite respect towards others are, however, defensible as signifying, to use the words of Pascal, " Je m' incommoderois bien, si vous en aviez besoin, puisque je le fais sans que cela vous serve." They are to be valued not so much for the advantage conferred, as for the sympathy, kindliness and goodwill that they express more clearly than words can do. Nor need such expressions of kindliness be condemned as deceitful, though, of course, like every other expression of feeling, they may be counterfeited for purposes of deceit. There is probably a great deal more of kindly sympathy in the world than can find expression, and, therefore, any means, by which the sympathy of man for man is expressed, works on the side of truth and helps to make our view of the world more in accordance with the facts. In this case knowledge is very conducive to happiness. For, as it is most miserable to suppose oneself the object of suspicion, hatred, or utter indifference, it is correspondingly pleasant to know that the world on the whole is sympathetic, and that an ordinary man, who does not act in such a way as to make himself peculiarly disagreeable, may

count upon the sympathy of his fellowmen, when he
is oppressed with grief and misfortune.

The mere expression of sympathy being conducive
to happiness, sympathy itself must take a high place
in utilitarian virtue. Anyone who increases the amount
of sympathy in the world may be sure that he is doing
good utilitarian work, the effect of which will go on
increasing like a sum of money lent out at compound
interest. For sympathy begets sympathy and equally
blesses him who gives and him who takes. It is as
pleasant to feel sympathy as to be the object of sympathetic feeling, and the example of sympathy is
contagious. Men who have been the objects of sympathy, or who have merely seen any striking example
of sympathy, are thereby disposed by the force of
example, or gratitude, to become sympathetic towards
others. The difficulty is to make the necessary beginning. How are we to increase the amount of sympathy
in the world ? Chiefly by being sympathetic ourselves.
But how are we to teach ourselves to be sympathetic ?
It is not easy to do this. The sympathetic man is born
rather than made. Yet within certain limits we may
train ourselves to sympathise with our fellowmen. If
we habitually try to help them in attaining their ends,
though at first we may be without sympathy, we shall
find ourselves gradually more and more sympathetic,
however slow may be the course of improvement. This
explains how it is that doctors sympathise more with
the pains of disease than ordinary men. They are so
constantly engaged in co-operating with sick persons,
in their efforts to get rid of disease, that they readily
identify themselves in feeling with all who suffer from ill
health. Another means of learning sympathy is to
suffer the pains for which our sympathy is needed, for
the poor sympathise most with the poor, the oppressed
with the oppressed. But as this process would involve
going out of one's way to incur pain it would be con-

demned by utilitarians as directly producing pain, though indirectly promoting happiness. Or, at any rate, such a plan can only be advocated as a means of promoting sympathy with the joys of others. By experiencing the joys of others we may cultivate a taste for their pleasures, which may increase the attractions of our companionship. But this is comparatively unimportant as sympathy is so much less necessary in joy than in pain.

A great deal of want of sympathy springs from contempt of our fellowmen. There is no doubt that the want of sympathy for women and negroes was due largely to the fact that they were despised as inferiors. So that the problem of increasing sympathy is to a large extent resolvable into the question whether we can eradicate our inclination to take pride in our fancied superiority over our fellowmen. This foolish pride is objectionable, not merely because it quenches sympathy, but also because it is painful to be despised, and ruinous to the moral nature to indulge in scorn, unless it be the scorn arising from indignation against vice. What then is the cure of scorn? It is not easily banished from the mind by mere effort of the will, nor is it easy to induce other men to cease to be scornful. Utilitarians, when they recognise the unhappiness caused by their contempt, both to themselves and to those whom they despise, may learn to abhor the feeling and so more or less subdue it.

But more can be done in this direction by religious influence than by moral considerations. Religion is much more teachable than morality to large masses of men. Christianity strongly inculcates such humility as is incompatible with contempt towards our fellowmen. All preachers, who by eloquence spread Christianity among the heathen or induce professing Christians to act more in accordance with the principles of their religion, contribute much to the happiness of the world by increasing humility, sympathy and moral conduct. For religion seems to suggest a satisfactory affirmative answer to the Socratic question : Can virtue be taught ? Christianity has been spread by teaching in nineteen centuries over a large fraction of the human race, and, wherever it has been established, men have learned the highest principles of morality, by carrying out which they are most likely to promote their own happiness, and that of others, and to sacrifice their own happiness to the greater happiness of others when those two ends conflict. Thus the acceptance of Christianity is as productive of happiness as the acceptance of the highest principles of morality, and has the advantage of being much more easily taught and more enthusiastically obeyed. Compare for instance the effect on the happiness of the world of Kant's categorical imperative on the one hand, and of the golden rule of Christianity on the other. The categorical imperative is no doubt more precise, and extends to a wider range of conduct than the golden rule. As Sidgwick points out, the golden rule is only applicable to our treatment of others, and, literally obeyed, might lead a man to commit crimes for others, if on reflection he found that he wished others to commit crimes for his benefit. Yet, practically, these objections are of no importance. The spirit, if not the letter, of the golden rule applies to our most self-regarding actions, and there is little likelihood of anyone who seriously tries to follow the precept being led thereby to commit vicious actions. Any objection, that might be made against it on the ground of its want of precision, is as nothing when compared with the fact that it is accepted as the utterance of God by millions of men, who are therefore strongly moved to obey it, not only for its moral excellence, but also because by so doing they both win for themselves everlasting happiness in a future life, and have the satisfaction of obeying, and, so far as they can, of furthering the purposes of a loving God.

This indeed is the great service that religion does

N

to the cause of happiness. Religion does not interfere
with the ordinary motives to morality, and adds to
them far stronger motives of its own. The man who
regards conscience as the voice of God in his soul
and finds the precepts of morality in his sacred books,
is far more powerfully impelled towards moral action,
than he who is only actuated by such motives as the
science of morality can give. Even the utilitarian,
however strongly he may be urged on to promote
happiness by sympathy with his fellowmen, will be
urged still more strongly to promote their happiness
if convinced that by so doing he is winning the approval and love of God. Of course this strong support
to morality can only be given by a religion which
is in accordance with the highest morality and can
adapt itself to the progress of humanity. Several
forms of religion, by binding themselves to unalterable
principles, have come into conflict with progressive
morality, and the result of the conflict has either been
retardation of moral progress or their own overthrow.
Christianity has proved its ability to keep pace with
the moral progress of nineteen centuries, and has itself
contributed immensely and is still contributing to that
progress. Above all, its moral principles are in perfect
harmony with utilitarianism, as its principal lesson is
the love of God for men, so that, if it contained any
precept, the literal obedience to which would in any
case diminish general happiness, the Christian would
be justified in supposing such precept to be given with
the understanding, that, though generally to be obeyed,
it was not to be obeyed when in conflict with the more
general principle, that man must, by every means, show
his love for God by loving his fellowmen. Thus utilitarianism and Christianity should return to the position
of alliance and mutual support in which they are found
in Paley's "Moral Philosophy."

S. Cowan & Co., Printers, Perth.